Thinking as You Play

SYLVIA COATS

Thinking as You Play

Teaching Piano in Individual and

Group Lessons

INDIANA UNIVERSITY PRESS
Bloomington and Indianapolis

This book is a publication of

Indiana University Press
601 North Morton Street
Bloomington, IN 47404-3797 USA

http://iupress.indiana.edu

Telephone orders   800-842-6796
Fax orders   812-855-7931
Orders by e-mail   iuporder@indiana.edu

The paper used in this publication meets the minimum requirements of American National Standard for Information Sciences—Permanence of Paper for Printed Library Materials, ANSI Z39.48-1984.

Manufactured in the United States of America

Library of Congress Cataloging-in-Publication Data

Coats, Sylvia Curry.
   Thinking as you play : teaching piano in individual and group lessons / Sylvia Coats.
      p. cm.
   Includes bibliographical references and index.
   ISBN 0-253-34676-2 (cloth : alk. paper) — ISBN 0-253-21815-2 (pbk. : alk. paper) 1. Piano—Instruction and study. I. Title.
   MT220.C72 2005
   786.2′193′071—dc22

                                                                              2005016229

1 2 3 4 5   11 10 09 08 07 06

To my students, who actually taught me.

To my teachers, who inspired me.

At the very least, a teacher is one who is at ease with shades of grey, one who pursues unrest marching toward excellence and one who is more alive than most. Certainly, not one who pursues the neurotic need of perfection.

Guy Duckworth, ". . . Reflections"

Contents

Preface and Acknowledgments   xi

1. Introduction   1
2. Lesson Planning   3
3. Developing Creativity through Student Discovery   19
4. The Real Basics of Music: Musical Concepts   28
5. The Real Basics of Music: Musical Principles   49
6. Designing a Curriculum   57
7. Communication between Student and Teacher   71
8. Learning Styles   94
9. Introduction to Group Teaching   106
10. Group Growth   112
11. Problem Solving in Group Lessons   117
12. Group Dynamics   133

Appendix 1. Dancing the Baroque Suites   147
Appendix 2. Features of Court Dance of the Renaissance and
      Baroque Periods   151
Appendix 3. Dancing and Playing the Romantic Dances   153
Bibliography   155
Index   159

Preface and Acknowledgments

This book is about how to teach piano. Its focus is on teaching individual and group lessons that go beyond learning the piece at hand to developing artistry through musical concepts, teaching problem-solving techniques, communicating through listening, and encouraging positive group dynamics.

The book is not an essay about pedaling, correct fingering, ornamentation, method selection, or the business of the studio. Other authors have ably covered these topics. The book is about the development of one's own pedagogy, which will in turn facilitate the selection of method books, styles of music, and effective approaches to reading and technique.

Most teaching is instructional. Little is said that will enable the students to transfer and absorb the concept into their daily practice. If students are to play with understanding and creativity, their practice must be thoughtful and musical. Teachers can learn principles for effective teaching just as the performer learns principles of music structure and interpretation. Once these principles are learned, the teacher's role transforms from that of mere instructor to facilitator of the student's discovery about the expressive relationships of musical concepts. We will look at what happens in a lesson, and how the teacher can design effective lessons in order to teach in a way that improves the student's practicing and learning.

The book is for piano teachers to study and apply principles of teaching to daily lesson problems. Experienced as well as beginning teachers and piano pedagogy students in college classrooms may benefit from this book. It represents my thoughts from thirty years of teaching, study, and assisting others in learning to teach piano. I have been a piano pedagogy and class piano teacher at universities for twenty-five years and have taught individual and group lessons in an independent studio for nearly forty years. My roles overlap because I teach college students to teach piano, college students to play piano as their second instrument, and children to play the piano at all levels of advancement. Because of this varied teaching background, I offer a narrative that combines performance practices, learning theory, and social and personal psychology for applications to piano lessons.

I will refrain from lengthy descriptions of what the experts in piano pedagogy, psychology, social science, and education have to say on these subjects other than to list recommended reading. Instead, descriptions of actual lessons with commentary will illustrate the topics. Principles of learning and teaching that can guide each lesson will be discussed.

I am deeply grateful to Dr. Guy Duckworth, my mentor and Professor Emeritus at the University of Colorado. He has been a role model as a teacher, an inspiration for playing the piano, a taskmaster who insisted that I do my best, and a pedagogical expert in giving advice about this book. The impact of his influence on my teaching will be evident throughout this book as I elaborate on ideas I learned from him.

I wish to thank Dr. John William Thomson, Chair of the School of Music at Wichita State University, for his encouragement, the Wichita State University piano faculty, my husband, Casey, and my children, Michelle and Jason, for their interest and support. Rebecca Shockley gave of her time to edit an early draft and Marienne Uszler gave insightful comments in her review.

To my students who invigorate my teaching I am especially appreciative. My writing is inspired by the graduate and undergraduate pedagogy students whose teaching I supervise. The students prepare lesson plans and provide commentary on the lesson; then, I observe a video of the lesson and evaluate their teaching effectiveness. These lessons provide food for thought as I write, and they give me real lessons for examples to explain the teaching process. I am grateful to numerous pedagogy students who have edited the draft as they have studied it in their classes. Thank you to Wendy Stevens for her help in formatting the musical examples. Thanks to my pre-college students, the reason I chose the rewarding profession of teaching the piano.

I hope piano teachers who read this book will find it helpful to improve their effectiveness as teachers. Pedagogical theory can be enormously helpful to teachers, and my aim is to make it accessible for daily use in your teaching.

Thinking as You Play

1   Introduction

Our goal as music teachers is to prepare students to understand music and to skillfully play an instrument so they can enjoy music for the rest of their lives. We want them to become proficient so they can continue to grow in their musical understanding. Therefore, how we teach the music becomes more important than the music or technology we use. Questions arise such as: How do children learn? How can teachers guide students to maximize their learning? How do we prepare students to take creative initiative in their musical interpretations? Inquiry into these questions is about the process of teaching.

The myriad of answers to these questions can be overwhelming. Students' learning styles are highly varied because each is a unique individual. The literature for piano is massive, and we can hardly make a dent in exposing students to the old legacy as well as the new.

As teachers, we need a way of thinking that gives us guidelines to solving daily lesson problems. We need to assist our students to make musical decisions independently. In order to assist the student in developing musical understanding, teachers need to have a process—teaching the concept, not just identifying the concept. The focus should be on the process of learning music, not on the product of music performance.

Most books on piano teaching focus on proper piano performance. However, this is not a book about proper technique or stylistic practice; rather, it is a book about how to get students to internalize concepts of music and think on their own—the process of learning. Learners have to be aware of the issues affecting their performance. Otherwise, students will become dependent on the teacher and never really know how they got from point A to point B.

Trust that students are their own best resource. Every student, child through adult, wants to learn, is capable of understanding complex concepts, and can solve problems on her own. As teachers we can unknowingly inhibit this process. If we think of students as vessels to be filled, then we may be unaware of reactions to the instruction that indicate the student's grasp of the material. By contrast, if we consider students to be their own best resource for learning, we can encourage students to become independent musicians.

Many piano teachers have learned social and personal psychology by experience. Teachers meet one-on-one for years with a student multiplied by twenty or more students a week. Such experienced teachers learn by doing. They instinctively know how to reach a student.

Others, particularly inexperienced teachers, may struggle with students who just don't get it. New teachers want to know what to teach. As they become reassured that a variety of method books are available for different ages, the focus then shifts to the presentation of new concepts and to practice motivation. Experienced teachers realize that improvement of teaching effectiveness is an ongoing process and they pursue professional development by visiting with colleagues, reading journals and books, and attending pedagogy workshops, classes, and conferences.

The pedagogical topics in this book are presented to experienced teachers as a guide to continued professional development and to inexperienced teachers as an introduction to teaching. The book is intended as a handbook to arm the teacher with an organized, creative approach to common issues in teaching individual and group lessons.

Principles of instruction are delineated to help the teacher focus on two levels of instruction: (1) the student's process and (2) the teacher's process. Chapters 2 through 8 are devoted to topics that will be useful for individual and group teaching. Chapter 2 stresses the importance of thinking about students before they come to the lesson and planning lessons that will enable consistent progress through engaging the student in musical activities. Chapter 3 presents a teaching philosophy to encourage student creativity by developing an attitude of taking risks and making educated guesses. Chapters 4 and 5 are the core of the book that emphasize concepts and principles of musical structure and interpretation. Suggestions are given to help teachers and students make interpretative choices. Chapter 6 gives guidelines for how to organize the music taught into a comprehensive curriculum. In Chapter 7, strategies of communication—what to say and how to say it—will help teachers become more effective in getting students to think and improve their practice and performance. Chapter 8 attempts to help teachers understand students' personalities by discussing students' preferred learning modalities and students' preferred learning styles, based on the Myers-Briggs type theory. This is particularly useful when the student does not comprehend the initial instruction and a different approach is needed.

The last four chapters focus on group teaching both for small groups of children and adults and large groups of university piano classes. Although examples are given from group lessons, the ideas are in most cases applicable to individual lessons as well. Chapter 9 serves as an overview of group teaching and gives suggestions for placing students in homogeneous groups. Chapter 10 is a fascinating topic of how groups grow and become productive. Chapter 11 offers a multitude of suggestions and focuses on the teacher's role and student's role in working effectively on musical problems. Several group lessons are evaluated to illustrate the topics discussed. Chapter 12 draws ideas from studies of groups and their effectiveness in order to assist the teacher in facilitating group lessons. The Appendixes offer information about the Baroque and Romantic dance forms.

I love to teach piano and piano pedagogy. The ideas presented in this book can be credited to my teachers and my students. What I have learned from them over the years has empowered me to keep learning from each teaching challenge that I encounter. I hope you will enjoy reading this book, and I hope you will be encouraged in your creativity as a teacher.

2   Lesson Planning

Students are different and in fact their needs change from one lesson to the next. As a result, learning approaches need to be flexible. Alicia wrote an insightful essay in a pedagogy class after her experience of teaching several students:

> I am realizing more and more that teaching is a lot like playing an instrument. Just like every piece of music should be approached from a new, fresh perspective, so a teacher should see each student as unique, and every lesson as an adventure. Because there are not definite rules of teaching that work with every student, teaching, like performing, should balance spontaneity with strategic planning. The way we teach should adapt and change with each and every student, just as the way that a musician plays will adapt and change depending on the particular piece he is studying.

Alicia has described an attitude about teaching that encourages an optimal experience of complete involvement and enjoyment by the student and teacher. Mihaly Csikszentmihalyi coined the flow model for optimal experience. He says flow begins when goals are clear and relate to student aspirations, challenge is just at or above a learner's ability level, and feedback is immediate, informative, and non-threatening. He describes a lesson using the flow model: "What particularly distinguished such teaching was a sense of timing and pace, an understanding of when to intervene and when to hold back, of how to turn mistakes into information that can lead to improvement" (187).

A sense of involvement, concentration, and enjoyment in the piano lesson characterizes the "good lesson." I recall days when I was very tired, but I felt no fatigue during lessons because teaching the student was energizing. James Mursell describes the developmental experience in music as "arresting" when it holds one's attention (101).

A sense of energy and intensity in a lesson doesn't just happen. It can be cultivated through thorough preparation and evaluation, yet carried out with an attitude of flexibility. In their second lesson Andrea noted Matt's confusion about key signatures and decided to teach him the Circle of Fifths. Matt, a college-age intermediate level student, was reluctant to learn it and for several lessons he was resistant to Andrea's instruction. His goal to play for enjoyment did not include learning theory. Andrea listened to him and started teaching theory through his music. Their lessons together evolved from a power struggle between Andrea's persistence and Matt's resistance to a more flexible interchange with Andrea modeling the sound and Matt attentively trying new ways of playing. This more dynamic relationship felt much more natural and productive to both of them.

The majority of teachers do not prepare a lesson plan in advance of an individual piano lesson. Lessons are scheduled one after the other and little time is available to make written notes of problems in the student's playing in order to prepare for the next lesson. By contrast, teachers often prepare plans for group lessons. Because the focus is on more than one student at a time, teachers plan the lesson in order to make the most of the time together.

I challenge the assumption that the individual lesson need not be planned. There has to be more involvement in the lesson than merely turning the pages of a method book. A teacher must have a teaching philosophy, a mission statement if you will, to enable her to guide the student to a deeper understanding of the music. The lesson plan provides an overview for each lesson that will enable the teacher to give direction to the lesson, yet at the same time provide flexibility according to the needs of the individual student.

In teaching piano pedagogy I find that lesson planning is a necessity for both beginning and experienced teachers. As I observe and supervise their teaching, their lesson plans provide me with information about what they teach and how they teach. Some plans are about the materials—what book and page number will be played and in what order. Others plan around a new concept to be learned such as the rhythm of a dotted quarter. Plans often center on a problem that a student had in a previous lesson such as legato pedaling. Seldom do they consider their method of delivery of the material and concepts. Will they ask questions, present a problem to be solved, tailor the approach to the student's learning style, or encourage discussion within a group? A plan for how to teach the musical concepts and repertoire is most important for effective instruction.

Teaching involves more than knowledge of music and teaching materials. Knowledge of how people learn and techniques to encourage cooperative learning are equally important in pedagogy training. Piano students need to learn how to learn so that they can make intelligent decisions about music they are playing. The development of the critical thinking skills of conceptualizing, analyzing, evaluating, and problem solving should be a major part of instruction.

In an integrated lesson the student will apply a concept learned in one piece to other pieces and technique exercises. The music used is secondary to teaching a student how to learn the music. Development of a student's practice habits, analytical thinking, and expressive playing are teaching goals to enable a student to practice and perform effectively. A lesson then is not about getting a student to learn a piece, but about getting the student to develop a learning process. Notice that the focus is on the student's learning, not the music or the teacher's knowledge of the piece.

Many times lessons are only sessions for correcting mistakes. The corrections require that the student be dependent on the teacher to find mistakes and correct them. Cynthia complained about Tiffany's progress after a year of lessons. She cited the student's lack of practice and her lack of concentration in lessons as possible sources of the problem. After observing Cynthia teach in a small practice room on campus, I noticed that she seemed to intimidate her young student by standing very close to her with pencil in hand, circling each mistake she made in her music. She said "not bad" if Tiffany pleased her rather than a positive phrase like "good rhythm." Sometimes lessons are only sessions to copy the teacher's interpretation of the music. The student becomes dependent on the teacher to make interpretive decisions. In both cases the focus is on the teacher and his knowledge. Unfortunately, because the student is entirely dependent on the teacher to learn the music, the student of such teaching may be unable to play the piano after lessons are discontinued.

In a student-centered lesson the communication between the student and teacher is characterized by questions about the student's perception of the music. Questions are conceptually based. As a student listens to a recording and studies the score, the teacher asks, "Are there repeated sections in this composition?" The question assesses if the student is listening and evaluating visual and aural information about the piece. Another question might be, "Where is the high point of the phrase?" The question asks the student to consider rhythmic, pitch, form, and dynamic information in order to answer. The teacher accepts the answers and builds on them by further justification from the music or asks more questions to guide the student to a more thoughtful answer. Collaborative discussion fosters students' confidence to make informed decisions about the music.

Planning a lesson is a consideration of possible ways to involve students in the decision making. Instead of plans consisting of a list of what is played when, the plan is a guide to possible problems that may occur in the music and musical concepts that may assist the student in solving the problems. By anticipating what issues may arise, the teacher plans questions that will guide the student to think about the music.

Teachers who plan materials and tasks to be accomplished often feel frustrated that there is not enough time to complete the agenda. A conceptual plan provides reinforcement of the concept in each composition played. Furthermore, the comparison of seeing the concept in other music will motivate the student to apply the concept to music practiced at home. Consider this principle: a concept used in similar yet different contexts enables the student to think independently in his practice. Therefore, there may not be time to hear all music and do all tasks that were planned, but the instructor should trust that the student can apply the concept learned to his practice with music not played in the lesson.

In Figure 2.1, a lesson design is suggested that will encourage opportunities for student insight. The topics touched on in this chapter are discussed more thoroughly in the following chapters. Planning a long-range curriculum for the semester or the year is discussed in Chapter 6. The lesson topics to be discussed in this chapter are (1) objectives of the lesson; (2) music and skills to explore concepts; (3) musical concepts stressed in the lesson; (4) a design for student discovery; (5) approach of who does what, when, and where; (6) communication; (7) adapting to students' learning styles; (8) pacing; and (9) evaluation.

Figure 2.1. Lesson Plan for Problem Solving

Objectives

Materials

Concepts in the problem(s) that may contribute to possible solutions

Concrete experiences to encourage problem solving and transfer of learning

    Limit conditions

    Symmetry: Transfer concept to other skills–sight read, transpose, improvise,
        memorize, harmonize

    Analogy: Eurythmics, singing, imagery

Approach: Who does what, when, and where

Teacher/student Interaction: Use a balance of praise, questions, lecture, and directions

Evaluation: Comments about the lesson

Objectives

What to teach and how to teach it are the focus of lesson plans. Consider the objectives of the lesson. Determine the musical concepts to be introduced such as introducing a new rhythm or dynamic marking or improving the skills of memorizing or sight reading. After the student plays, consider possible problems that may need work such as continuity, phrasing, or accuracy to further define the objectives of the lesson.

In a supervised teaching course with me the following student teachers listed lesson objectives. Jim's plan of objectives for Melissa, an engineering major, was to (1) polish "In a Hammock" for the mid-term exam by discussing phrasing and dynamics; and (2) discuss principles of sight reading (Fig. 2.2).

Lanelle began the semester by planning what music would be played with no overall objectives in mind (Fig. 2.3), but she ended the semester by planning how she would teach the music and listed objectives for her student, Alex (Fig. 2.4).

Claire's objectives for a group of elementary-aged boys were ambitious: (1) review whole steps, half steps, sharps/flats, major and minor pentachords; (2) ear training: hearing and playing intervals, short melodies; (3) melodic direction; and (4) improvising/composing and performing (Fig. 2.5).

For elementary level students, determine the new concepts that will be introduced in the method book assignment. Often the concept is reinforced through

Figure 2.2. Jim's Lesson Plan Using Imagery

Teacher: Jim

Student: Melissa, a college engineering major

Lesson Objective

- Review and polish "In a Hammock," discussing phrasing, dynamics, and other elements

- Discuss principles of sight reading

Possible Questions

- Have you ever been in a hammock?

- Describe that feeling.

- Transfer that to the piece.

- What do you think of when you approach a new piece?

Transfer/Analogy

- Imagery

- Movement

- Singing

Jim's evaluation of the lesson follows. "Wow! The imagery was quite successful in making the transfer to the music. Good comments with sight reading. She really got confirmation that she could and can do it."

reading, listening, and written theory activities. More than one concept may be introduced.

For intermediate level students, objectives may be to develop fluid, fast playing; polishing a composition for a performance; developing sight reading skills; or projecting a melody above an accompaniment.

Materials

The sound of the music is what motivates the student to play. Nurturing the excitement and satisfaction of playing music is a teacher's ultimate goal. The

Figure 2.3. Lanelle's Plan of Materials at the Beginning of the Semester

Teacher: Lanelle

Student: Alex, thirteen years old

Material: Sonatina Album

- Choose two pieces

- Point out the form, dynamics, how to practice

- Sight read some of the music

Scales

- One or two octaves hands together or separate

- Group 1 white keys

Chords

- Group 1 chord progression

choice of repertoire should appeal to the student and teacher. The musical concepts to be taught will be similar no matter what music is taught. Develop a
curriculum that encompasses scales, chords, theory, harmony, and creativity
through improvisation and composition as well as a reading method and repertoire. In planning the materials to be used in the lesson, consider repertoire,
theory including scales and chords, and technical exercises that will contribute
to the student's understanding of the lesson objectives. For instance, if minor
scales are introduced, look for music in minor keys so that the student has opportunities to hear music in minor as well as play scales in minor.

Concepts

What musical concepts will contribute to understanding the objectives
of the lesson? For a beginning student the focus will be to reinforce the concepts
that were learned in previous lessons and to introduce new concepts from the
lesson book. Beginning methods used today have excellent reinforcement of a
new concept between the lesson, theory, and technique books. For instance, if
the interval of a sixth is introduced in the lesson book, the theory book will
have exercises in recognizing and writing sixths, the technique book will have
exercises and etudes in the fingering for sixths, and repertoire books will extend
the hand beyond the interval of a fifth. This conceptual approach to using the

Figure 2.4. Lanelle's Plan of How to Teach the Materials at the End of the Semester

---

Teacher: Lanelle

Student: Alex, thirteen years old

Objectives

- Memorization, articulation

Materials

- Mozart Sonata K. 545, II, second half of piece

- Dussek sonatina, second movement

- Review for final exam, three forms of minor scales and cadences

- Schubert Impromptu

Concepts in the problem

- Pitch patterns, key, tempo, articulation

Transfers of Learning

- Sight read different period styles with appropriate articulation

Approach

- Memorize in block chords, backwards, and study the key relationships.

- Emphasize clarity of touch and a variety of tone qualities.

Teacher/student Interaction

- How many different ways are there to memorize?

- Which one works best for you?

- Lecture that very slow memory practice, hands alone is another good way to practice.

Evaluation of the lesson

---

method books is also a good model for planning materials with more experienced intermediate and advanced students. For instance, the objective of playing sixteenth notes evenly can be reinforced by practicing scales, arpeggios, and scale passages in a sonatina.

In the lesson with the group of boys mentioned in Figure 2.5, Claire listed

Figure 2.5. Claire's Plan for a Children's Group

Teacher: Claire

Students: Four elementary-aged boys

Problem

    Review whole steps, half steps, sharps/flats, major and minor pentachords

    Ear training: hearing and playing intervals, short melodies

    Melodic direction

    Improvising/composing and performing

Materials

    Joanne Haroutounian's *Explorations in Music*

Concepts/Principles

    Knowing major and minor pentachord patterns

    Aural skills

    Dynamic contrast

    Handling nervous feelings and creating beautiful music

Transfer of Learning and Approach to the Problem

    Discuss and play half steps and whole steps (sharps/flats)

    Identify the difference between major/minor and sing/play the two forms

    Listen, sing, and play short melodies for one another

    Create spontaneous melodies and dictate them

    Perform for one another and discuss the performance

Continued on the next page

the following concepts and skills to accomplish the objectives: (1) knowing major and minor pentachord patterns; (2) aural skills; (3) dynamic contrast; and (4) handling nervous feelings and creating beautiful music.

An effective lesson integrates many musical concepts into solving a particular problem. For instance, if a student has difficulty reading with continuity, several

Figure 2.5. *Continued*

Teacher/student Interaction

    Ask open-ended questions to discuss the review of material

    Let the students teach one another in pairs

    Give them things to listen for and have them evaluate what they heard

Evaluation

    Claire commented, "The group enjoyed their interaction. They were challenged to think about the music in terms that we had been working with while still being spontaneous and creative."

---

solutions might be tried, each one focusing on one concept or an integration of several concepts. The student might try a slow tempo with the metronome, counting aloud to encourage looking ahead, or shaping the phrase by finding the high point to give direction to the music. Other concepts that may assist the student in successfully playing the new rhythm are note values already learned, patterns within a meter, and a slow tempo.

Also important to teaching conceptually is highlighting the concept through skills such as improvising and transposing. In teaching the interval of a sixth mentioned earlier, have the student sing and improvise a melody using the leap of a sixth and notice the natural tendency to follow the leap with stepwise motion. Harmonize a melody using fifths and sixths: the tonic chord shell, C and G, and the dominant chord shell, B and G.

Figure 2.6 is a lesson plan given to seven-year-olds in their first piano lesson. Notice the emphasis on concepts through composing songs and improvising on the rhythms of folk tunes.

Concrete Experience

When students have a concrete experience with a new concept, they must actively think. What they have experienced they will more than likely remember and use in other music. Thus, they will transfer the learned concept to new situations. Provide experiences at the lesson to help the student understand the new concept. Anticipate ways to encourage the student to make intuitive leaps of understanding.

Three guidelines for developing intuitive thinking are:

1. Limit the conditions of what is played
2. Use analogies of singing, moving, or imagery

Figure 2.6. Plan for the First Piano Lesson

Objectives

Getting to know one another through music. Learning about melody and rhythm

Materials

Make up a song. Improvise on the rhythm of "Twinkle, Twinkle, Little Star," "Humpty Dumpty," "Jack and Jill"

Concepts

Make up song: melody, rhythm, imitation, loud-soft, smooth-detached, fast-slow

Improvisations: melody–up, down, same, steps, skips, repeats

Pulse–beat, continuity (with walking the beat)

Rhythm–short, long, quarter, half, two eighths (clapping the rhythm)

Principles

Melodies have sounds that are high and low; rhythms that are long or short; and a speed of the beat that remains the same

Concrete experiences to encourage transfer of learning

Analogy

Singing, shaping melodies in the air

Moving the feet to the beat and clapping the rhythm

Imagining a story for made-up piece

Symmetry

Improvise

Figure 2.6. *Continued*

Approach

Students help each other learn

Challenge them to think

Get to know one another

Teacher/student Interaction

Ask questions, encourage, and build on students' ideas

Give directions, make conduct rules, lecture on what was learned about melody and
   rhythm

Make Assignment

---

3. Use symmetry of similar skills such as reading, transposing, harmonizing, playing by ear, or improvising

Limiting the conditions of what is played to enable the student to be successful
may be as simple as choosing one phrase of the music or perhaps one hand.
Analogies to playing the piano that assist intuitive thinking are singing the
melody or scale; moving to the rhythm by clapping, directing, or dancing; and
using imagery of moods, colors, pictures, or stories to describe the music. In
Jim's lesson with Melissa mentioned in Figure 2.2, he used the imagery of lying
in a hammock to help her play expressively. Lanelle used *symmetry* to help Alex
understand the touch needed in a Bach Prelude by having him sight read in different style periods (Fig. 2.4). She directed him to contrast the detached articulation of the Baroque style with the pedaled sound of the Romantic style.

A good rule of thumb is to learn by doing rather than by telling. Instead of
lecturing about the concept, involve the student in an activity using the concept.

Approach

This area of the lesson plan concerns the choreography of the lesson—
who will do what and when. To encourage cooperative learning, plan for students to sit in a circle to sing songs or clap rhythms. To focus on hand position,
invite all students to view and discuss each person's hand position and posture.
In Figure 2.5, Claire's approach to the boys' group lesson was:

- Discuss and play half steps and whole steps (sharps/flats)
- Identify the difference between major/minor and sing/play the two forms
- Listen, sing, and play short melodies for one another
- Create spontaneous melodies and dictate them
- Perform for one another and discuss the performance

In the individual setting the teacher may plan to hear all music before commenting. She may start the lesson with a duet to get the student in the mood for music after a busy day at school or work. The use of technology may be a strategy to help students evaluate and find solutions to musical problems. Have students listen to recordings, play with CD accompaniments to method books, or record a performance using a video recorder or a computer-sequencing program.

Communication

Telling is not as effective as asking questions to get students to think. Telling students the facts of rhythm values, note names, or modeling the interpretation of the music does not help the student conceptualize, analyze, and think on his own in practice. Asking questions that lead him to think will encourage him to think in the practice room. Because traditional instruction has not often involved asking questions as a primary mode of delivery, plan questions that you might ask in order to lead the student to understand the objectives of the lesson. Be sure to respond to the student's answer. Questions and responses lead to a more in-depth discussion of the topic with the student.

Jim was not in the habit of asking questions, so he planned the following questions and directions to ask Melissa about "In a Hammock" (Fig. 2.2).

Possible Questions

- Have you ever been in a hammock?
- Describe that feeling.
- Transfer that to the piece.
- What do you think of when you approach a new piece?

In Figure 2.5, Claire listed ideas for interaction within the group lesson and evaluated the results: (1) ask open-ended questions to review the material; (2) let the students teach one another in pairs; and (3) have them prepare things to listen for and then evaluate what they heard. Claire commented, "The group enjoyed their interaction. They were challenged to think about the music in terms that we had been working with while still being spontaneous and creative."

Learning Styles

Students may have a preference for a particular mode of learning—visual, auditory, or kinesthetic. Other students work well in all learning modes. Observe the student's preference and adapt the presentation to help him. Each lesson can be planned with activities that vary between seeing the music, hearing the music, and moving to the music.

Knowledge about individual learning styles will assist the teacher to provide effective instruction. Some students may be stimulated to think by interacting with their peers, while others may need a quiet space to think through a concept. Some learn by doing, and others prefer to think more abstractly. Fortunately, help is available to develop flexibility in adapting to students' individual learning styles (Chapter 8).

Pacing

Teachers may want to plan the order of what is played at the lesson—technique, the books and page numbers that will be played, theory or musical games, and performance preparation for a recital or festival. Experiment with the order and pacing to encourage the student's maximum involvement throughout the lesson. Some students need a routine that will prompt them to practice in an efficient way. Other students may need variety in the lesson format. If a student bursts into the lesson declaring that she has a piece to play, that enthusiasm deserves top billing, so by all means hear it first.

Strive to have an intensity of purpose in each lesson. Consider the length of the lesson and the duration of each part of the lesson. Does the lesson develop a momentum that encourages concentration and active involvement throughout the lesson?

Evaluation

Soon after the lesson write an evaluation citing the student's progress and plans for the next lesson. Note effective and ineffective strategies with the student. List new music that may be assigned.

Keep in mind that lesson plans are made to be broken. If the student has practiced a Beethoven Sonata but you planned to work on a Chopin Prelude, by all means work on the Sonata. The lesson will be more fruitful because you spent the time and effort to really think about the individual student, even though you didn't follow your plan. More than likely, if the plan was conceptual, you may address the issues you planned anyway. Concepts of phrasing, pedaling, fingering, and so on are issues to be addressed in all music. Helping students develop good habits in one piece at the lesson will transfer to other music that he will play in practice.

In order to review one's teaching effectiveness an occasional video of a lesson taught will help that assessment. Figure 2.7, Assessment Tool for the Care and Nurture of the Piano Student, was an instrument used in my piano pedagogy class for student teachers to review their teaching as well as for classmates to review their peers. An assessment instrument serves to remind one of factors important in the lesson as well as being a measure of the effectiveness of a specific lesson.

Figure 2.7. Assessment Tool for the Care and Nurture of the Piano Student

Care and Nurture of the Piano Student

Checklist for Teaching

Problem Solving

- Teacher assesses student's problem adequately.

- Student is told what concept is being stressed.

- Student tries out suggestions at lesson.

- Teacher asks questions to see if student understands.

- Student improves her playing.

- Student is led to make decisions about music independently.

Materials

- Music is the appropriate level for the student.

- A curriculum is used of scales, chords, theory, harmony, and creativity through improvisation and composition.

- Elementary students have comprehensive method books; intermediate students have a variety of musical styles.

Concepts and Principles

- Teacher has a conceptual focus on musical elements and applies the learned concept to other music.

- Teacher allows student to apply one concept before requiring others to be perfected.

Figure 2.7. *Continued*

Intuitive Thinking and Transfer of Learning

- Student is prepared for success by limiting the conditions for playing.

- Teacher uses a variety of functional skills to reinforce musical concepts.

- Movement, singing, and imagery help the student understand concepts.

Approach

- Teacher helps student to fully concentrate on piano playing.

- Teacher provides concrete experiences for learning music.

- Student spends the majority of the lesson playing and discussing. Teacher gives cues, directions, and models to assist learning with a minimum of talk.

- Teacher uses technology to assist learning: accompaniment disks; performance, theory, composition software; Internet sites.

- Teacher is aware of student's learning style and adapts instruction as needed.

Teacher Influence

- Teacher talk is balanced between dominative, direct influence (telling, directing, and critiquing) and integrative, indirect influence (questioning, praising, accepting feelings, and using student ideas).

- Teacher values ideas of student.

- Teacher shows genuine concern and respect for the student as a person.

- Teacher shares enthusiasm about music.

Continued on the next page

Figure 2.7. *Continued*

Group Dynamics

- Students cooperated rather than competed and learned from one another.

- Students felt success and a sense of self-esteem.

- Group interaction helped students understand the concept and play successfully.

Suggested Reading

Baker-Jordan, *Practical Piano Pedagogy.*
Csikszentmihalyi, Rathunde, and Whalen, *Talented Teenagers.*
Mursell, *Education for Musical Growth.*

Further Thought

- Describe a lesson that you have taken as a student or given as a teacher that was a "state of flow."
- Discuss the advantages and disadvantages of making a lesson plan.
- List possible objectives for (1) a beginning student's lesson, (2) an intermediate student's lesson.
- Describe what a teacher does in a teacher-centered lesson; in a student-centered lesson.
- Why is it important to encourage students to think intuitively rather than only to memorize facts?

3   Developing Creativity through Student Discovery

Music touches the emotions. It makes us more fully human. One's primary reason for studying music is to enrich one's soul. Music provides solace in times of grief and enrichment in our everyday lives.

The pursuit of self-expression is a goal for the student in the first year of study as well as for the accomplished artist-performer. Therefore, the teaching approach should encourage creativity. Beginning piano methods present primarily the facts of musical study—the grand staff, note values, and dynamic signs. It is up to the teacher to present the method in a way that encourages the student to think creatively.

This chapter offers ideas about a learning environment that promotes:

• Guessing and exploration
• A rhythm of musical growth
• Intuitive thinking
• Critical thinking

Guessing and Exploration

A teacher can encourage the student to trust his intuition and to make educated guesses. One can arrive at a plausible solution without analyzing the situation. Jerome Bruner says, "Intuitive thinking, the training of hunches, is a much-neglected and essential feature of productive thinking not only in formal academic disciplines but also in everyday life" (13–14). Bruner suggests that intuitive thinking can be taught. With an affective discipline such as music, training in intuitive thinking is key to developing creativity.

Children know more about music than teachers think they do. Their knowledge about music may be intuitive, so they might not be able to verbalize what they know. If the child does try to verbalize her understanding, she may say the music is happy, sad, or scary. A teacher can probe further and the child may elaborate on musical properties: "The happy music was fast and loud." Because a child's natural response to music is intuitive, the approach to teaching music should be one that nurtures creativity.

Rather than a bottom-up approach to teaching that starts with the building blocks of music—note names, rhythm names, time signatures—I propose a top-down approach that starts with the global properties of music—higher-lower, faster-slower, louder-softer. Children gleefully make up music to experiment with the sound of the piano. Their imaginative music depicts a thunderstorm, or a soccer game, or a playful kitten. They naturally demonstrate "the global properties of music" of higher and lower, faster and slower, and louder and softer.

In most beginning music lessons, sound is presented as a new fact to learn: the location of middle C on the piano and the grand staff or the value of quarter and half note rhythms. Instead, the teacher can involve the student in a direct experience of the global properties of music through singing melodies and moving to rhythms before she knows the facts of middle C and quarter note. After the direct experience, the teacher can guide her to analyze the music and discover the facts of pitch direction, rhythmic lengths, and dynamic signs. The approach begins with an experience of music and moves to an analysis of music.

The top-down approach encourages music to be felt and enjoyed. Howard Gardner, in his theory of the seven intelligences, includes a musical intelligence: "[W]hen scientists finally unravel the neurological underpinnings of music— reasons for its effects, its appeal, its longevity—they will be providing an explanation of how emotional and motivational factors are intertwined with purely perceptual ones" (106). However, Gardner rightly points out that any individual who wants to gain musical competence should master music analysis.

Developing musical competence can begin with an intuitive feeling for the music and move to an analysis of the music. Let children sing melodies and explore the keyboard to find the melody. As they match pitches by trial and error they discover important facts about a melody: pitch direction of higher and lower and interval distance of step and skip. Students can clap to the pulse of the music and then move and clap showing the difference between quarter and half note rhythms. After they feel the rhythm in their bodies, they quickly understand the symbols representing pitch and rhythm. They don't yet know the names of the notes or rhythms, but they have intuitively grasped information about musical elements. If the student had been told what notes to play and how many beats to count each note, he would have missed the fundamental features of sound—melody and movement.

A teaching approach should focus on the global properties of music and its expressivity. Such an approach embodies exploration and discovery, tolerance for mistakes, trying several solutions, guessing, and trusting oneself.

Rhythm of Learning

Discovery learning seems consistent with cognitive theory about how people learn and develop. Both Bruner and Jean Piaget identify stages of cognitive growth. First the child comes to understand through his actions—listening and trying out sounds. Then he moves to identification of the symbols. Discovery learning allows students to move through this process when they encounter new information. Mursell identifies a continuum of the rhythm of learning (Table 3.1). "It [musical growth] is a movement from crudeness toward precision, from the concrete toward the abstract, from the immediate toward the universal, from vagueness toward clarity, from hesitation toward certainty" (73).

Table 3.1

Rhythm of Musical Growth
Concrete to Abstract
Immediate to Universal
Crude to Precise
Vague to Clear
Hesitant to Certain

According to Mursell, movement from one end of the spectrum to the other must center upon musical content, musical expressiveness, and musical responsiveness (91). Guy Duckworth, Professor Emeritus at the University of Colorado, who studied with Mursell, warns that if the teacher interrupts this natural process of student musical growth—particularly when goals are vague—and attempts to impose clarity, the likely result will be dependent student behavior ("Notes on Group," 102). To avoid interrupting the process, instructors should refrain from immediately correcting the mistake. Instead, the teacher should ask questions and build on the student's answer to get the student to think about the problem and to explore solutions for himself.

The rhythm of musical growth is on a continuum from the start of learning the subject matter to the end of the process. A child sings "Hot Cross Buns" and plays it by ear on the black keys. The child learns through this "concrete" experience. His attempts to find the melody are at first "crude and imprecise," but as he explores the relation of the keyboard to his singing, he finds the notes of the melody and is able to perform the melody accurately. What began as crude becomes precise. The teacher then explains that melodies are built on scales with varying intervals, pitches, and rhythms. The student's "concrete" experience led to an "abstract" understanding of melodic intervals and rhythms. The student's "immediate" need was to learn to play a song, but the abstraction is a "universal" understanding of how melodies are composed and leads to the possibility that he can learn other melodies in a similar way.

At the outset of learning the melody goals were vague. The student wasn't sure what to do or if he could play the melody. As he correctly identified passages of the melody, his goal became "clear" and he worked until he found all the notes of the melody. His "hesitancy" evolved into "certainty." If the teacher had interrupted this process by naming the correct notes and doing the work for the student, the student might not have been able to pick out another melody. His exploration of learning how to identify a melody would have been interrupted.

To develop intellectual and emotional abilities, one has to guess, make mistakes, try again, and find one's own solution. Therefore, there are times in the process when learning is messy and noisy, not clear and precise. Alexis and Cody, elementary students in a partner lesson, are learning to make educated guesses about music. New concepts are presented to them and then they experiment at the piano to discover more about the concept. This takes a willingness to explore and make mistakes in order to gain insight into the concept. For example, in one lesson the children were learning the difference between major and minor. They had been singing and playing melodies built on major five-finger scales for six weeks, and at this lesson they were asked to play a minor melody after singing it. Each child worked on their own matching pitches they had sung, but they realized the sound of the third of the scale was not quite right. Jack, the teacher, asked questions to guide them to listen to the third note of the scale and gave them the suggestion of trying the black keys as well as the white. Both children enjoyed experimenting and both found the minor scale and played the melody.

A teacher unknowingly may not complete the process to arrive at clarity. Following is a description of a lesson by a student-teacher that provides an example of an incomplete rhythm of learning. John's student Misha was reviewing the Beethoven Sonata, Op. 10, No. 1 for a recital performance. She played unmusically so he directed her not with words but through conducting and modeling, to crescendo for phrase tension and soften for phrase endings. This is an effective approach; however, after Misha's successful playing he failed to summarize or have her verbalize what principles of phrasing made her playing so musical. Identifying what causes more tension in a phrase such as dissonance, and the resolution to consonance that releases the tension would have enabled Misha to apply the principle during her practice. The most effective lessons move from vagueness to clarity. If what is learned at a lesson isn't reviewed and verbalized by the student, the experience will remain vague and it is doubtful that their practice will embrace what was learned.

When both teacher and student have an awareness of the natural rhythm of musical growth, expectation of that growth sustains appreciation for the process even when the going gets rough.

Intuitive Thinking

Table 3.2 gives three suggestions to help students develop intuitive thinking. After the student performs, the instructor should provide a concrete experience to improve the student's playing. These suggestions provide ideas for planning concrete experiences.

To create ideal conditions for a student to gain insight, a problem is limited so that the student can be challenged and successful rather than frustrated and defeated. Limit the amount of music played, such as to one measure, phrase, or section. Limit the number of corrections made in lessons and instead focus on one or two concepts to emphasize the correction. Lanelle observed that her teenage student, Alex, had forgotten what they worked on the week before. He played the "Spinning Song" by Ellmenreich too fast without expression or proper bal-

Table 3.2

Developing Intuitive Thinking
1) Limit conditions for playing
2) Use analogies of singing, moving, and imagery
3) Use symmetry of similar skills such as reading, transposing, harmonizing, playing by ear, improvising

ance of melody and accompaniment. She commented that maybe she had given too many directions in the previous lesson. She decided to focus on the concept of balance and had Alex play the melody while marking the accompaniment (touching the keys but not playing out loud). Lanelle also worked on balance in the Burgmuller "Pastoral." Alex understood her focus after working on the two pieces, and from that point forward he played music he sight read with good balance.

In a lesson with Hua-Ling, Lanelle had her memorize by chord analysis and blocking broken chords in Mozart's Sonata K. 545. She analyzed chords in other music and played cadences in various keys, which reinforced a harmonic memory. Lanelle provided lessons fertile with possibilities for "aha" moments for her students.

Analogous activities such as imagery, singing, and eurhythmics expand the student's understanding. Cynthia trained her student, Natalie, to sing the words as she practiced her pieces so that she would play with continuity and sense the flow of the phrase. Natalie played her piece beautifully at the recital, and much to her teacher's surprise she sang the words with gusto.

Using analogies is beneficial to both beginning and advanced students of all ages. In the previous chapter we mentioned Jim's lesson with Melissa on polishing "In a Hammock." Rather than telling her specific measures for soft and loud, he began by asking questions. "Have you ever been in a hammock? Describe that feeling." Melissa responded that she had enjoyed having a hammock at her home while she was growing up. Jim asked her to apply her feelings to the piece. She played with a lovely legato and shaped the phrase from *piano* to *mezzoforte* with a gentle ending. She was pleased with her sound and Jim then told her what dynamics she had used. A strategy that ensures retention is to encourage the student to play with imagination and then analyze what was done.

Another analogous activity is to move to the pulse of music to help students internalize the feeling of rhythm. It is impossible to conceptualize rhythm as movement through time without a physical representation, not just a factual one. Alicia had her group of two students, Nathaniel and Julie, clap and count quarter, half, whole, dotted quarter, dotted half, and eighth notes with the metronome. Then she had each child draw different rhythmic patterns on a white board for the other student to clap and count. In the next lesson Nathaniel and Julie were having trouble staying together in a duet. Alicia had them walk the beats while clapping the rhythm. She also asked them to alternate playing two measures of the duet so they had to listen and feel the pulse to start in time. The listening and eurhythmic activities developed the students' critical listening abilities.

I have taught the dance steps to the Baroque dances for many years. It always amazes me that after dancing the minuet or gigue that the students are studying, they intuitively change articulations, ornaments, and dynamics to more clearly capture the style of the dance. Experiencing the full body movement of the dance enables the students to internalize the sense of the dance that mental practice does not (see the appendixes).

Symmetrical activities such as functional skills of reading, transposing, harmonizing, playing by ear, and improvising allow concepts learned to be transferred to similar yet different situations. Emphasizing similarities in music helps students delve into the inner contents of the composition and assists them in developing an understanding of what the composer is communicating. Several college-class piano texts for beginners introduce major and minor five-finger scales, provide several examples for reading and transposing music in different five-finger scales, and provide teacher accompaniments while students improvise in five-finger patterns. Playing the scales using these functional skills helps the student understand the concept through symmetrical activities.

Mary Ann introduced the tetrachords in a major scale to a class of college music majors. They played the tetrachord divided between hands in several major keys; they analyzed a Beethoven piece using the D major scale; they played "Joy to the World" by ear and noted the descending scale pattern; and they improvised melodies based on scale tones. Mary Ann focused on the musical expressiveness by emphasizing the melodic contour and by pointing out moving and resting scale tones.

Students can learn to conceptualize with the practice aids of limiting the conditions for playing and by using analogous and symmetrical activities. These practice aids can enhance a student's intuitive thinking and thus increase the possibilities for insightful transfers.

Problem Solving—Critical Thinking

A major priority in piano teaching is to motivate the student to practice effectively. How can we teach in a way that will enable the student to go to the practice room and know what to do? Getting the students to think critically about their playing in the lesson will help them apply similar thinking to their practice.

Often called problem solving, the process is a progression in which the teacher

Table 3.3

Problem Solving
Presentation and/or awareness of the problem
Student definition of the problem
Experimentation with possible solutions
Verification of the solution

presents a musical problem, helps the student identify the problem, directs the student to experiment at the piano to find a solution, and helps the student verify the solution to the problem. Marienne Uszler provides a discussion of the process in *The Well-Tempered Keyboard Teacher* (248–252). Table 3.3 is patterned after her discussion.

Problem solving is not just finding mistakes and making corrections. It is a process of higher-level thinking that can empower students to learn on their own. By frequently modeling this process in the lesson, the teacher can motivate the student to make problem solving a part of the practice process. Let's begin first with how the teacher can use the problem-solving process in a lesson.

Consider the usual scenario in a lesson: a student plays a passage inaccurately and the teacher corrects it. Does the student do the work or does the teacher do the work? If the teacher gives the answer and the student passively follows the directions, it's likely that he will not remember the correction in his practice. Adam pointed out to Ben, an eighth-grade student, that his rhythm was inaccurate in a passage of the Clementi Sonatina in C Major, Op. 55, No. 3. Adam set the metronome at a slow tempo (eighth note at 96) and had him play again with little success. Adam counted for him and modeled the correct rhythm, but Ben still had inaccurate rhythm. Adam presented the problem, but Ben was never sure which note rhythms he was playing incorrectly. He dutifully followed Adam's directions, but never really thought about what the problem was and what he might do to correct it.

Following is a scenario of what Adam might do if he used the problem-solving process.

- Tell him what passage was incorrect (presentation of the problem).
- Help him realize exactly what rhythms he missed (student identification of the problem).
- Let him count to correct his mistake.
- Have him write in the counts and ask him questions about the note values.

- Practice for a few minutes, using the metronome (experimenting with possible solutions).
- Play correctly and confidently (verification).

I suggested to Adam that he help Ben identify the problem, but then get out of the way to see if the student could work out the rhythm independently.

In a later lesson with Ben, Adam did a good job of identifying specific problem passages in the Sonatina and led Ben to polish notes, rhythms, and especially phrasing. Ben played well as they worked through the piece. However, when Adam asked him to play the piece again, Ben did not incorporate the changes. He did not "verify" that the solutions would be lasting. Adam wisely had him pencil in the changes. Training students to think and become aware of what they are doing takes patience and persistence. Seeing the student grow to love music and play with creativity is well worth the effort.

Advancing students should be held accountable for accurate practice so that corrections at the lesson are minimized. At the intermediate level of study the student is expected to play with accurate notes, rhythms, and dynamics and attend to the balance of melody and accompaniment. Madeleine, an eighth-grade student playing the Heller Etude, Op. 47, No. 19, effectively brought out the melody with fingers 2, 3, 4, and 5, while softening the repeated-note accompaniment in the thumb of the right hand. At the same lesson she played a piece from the Faber *Technique and Artistry,* Level 3A, with a similar right-hand figure with tenuto marks highlighting the melody. Madeleine did not perform it correctly. I mentioned it to her and she acted embarrassed: she realized she wasn't concentrating and listening. After I mentioned it, she immediately played well without my having to spend extra time in the lesson showing her how to play it.

Allowing students to work through solving a problem often illuminates holes in their understanding. Adam's student Megan, an eleven-year-old playing in the second level of a method book, was rather lazy and quite dependent on Adam to teach her notes and rhythms in her music. He often counted with her in the lessons. When he let Megan count on her own, he realized that she did not understand how to count eighth notes and he was able to get at the root of Megan's rhythm problem.

Training students to learn music conceptually is essential for critical thinking (see Chapter 4). Although the advancing student should be encouraged to incorporate the problem-solving process into daily practice, the beginning student can be exposed to the process through the teacher's model. After presenting a new concept or exploring a problem part, the teacher may ask the student to define what the problem was (identification of the problem), state how the problem was solved, and try the solution with other music (verification of the problem). This strategy of teaching encourages students to use their intuition to make educated guesses. It is really a process that encourages students to "learn how to learn."

Every student is unique and thus no two students can be taught in exactly the same manner. In order to help students find and use their creativity, teachers must have an arsenal of approaches to assist them. Teaching requires exhaustive thought and effort, but the rewards are well worth it when a student plays confidently and expressively in a performance or a student beams with pride at a composition he has written.

Imagine a student on stage playing a piano and violin recital with confidence, enjoying the music, creating interpretations of her music that are musically expressive and stylistic with technical ease. Her piano teacher joins her for the final piece, the Saint-Saëns Piano Concerto No. 2. They are transported by the beautiful music. She takes a bow to a crowd who stand to congratulate her and thank her for touching their hearts with her playing. Her smile is appreciative, but her enjoyment of the music and her accomplishment are what please her most. She continues her musical growth in college by playing chamber music and joining the orchestra. Her teacher reflects on the many years of lessons they have shared together and appreciates the discoveries they have made about the music and each other. The teacher is assured that her student's musical understanding is built on the inner essence of music and that she will continue to play and learn literature as she prepares for and enters a career in the medical field.

Suggested Reading

Bruner, *Process of Education.*
Duckworth, "Notes on Group Performance Instruction in the Studio."
Gardner, *Frames of Mind.*
Green and Lehrer, *The Inner Game of Music Solo Workbook for Piano.*
Mursell, *Education for Musical Growth.*
Piaget and Inhelder, *The Psychology of the Child.*
Uszler, Gordon, and Smith, *The Well-Tempered Keyboard Teacher.*
Westney, *The Perfect Wrong Note.*

Further Thought

- What are the global properties of music?
- Give examples using intuition in learning.
- Describe the rhythm of learning something new.
- List analogies to playing.
- What is the difference between problem solving and correcting mistakes?

4 The Real Basics of Music: Musical Concepts

Why do some performances stand out and others are forgettable? I pondered this question after I heard several students play in a festival. A middle-school-aged student played a very expressive performance of "Curious Story," Op. 15, No. 2 by Robert Schumann. A high school student played a rather dull performance of "Impromptu," Op. 90, No. 3 by Franz Schubert. Both students were well prepared with the music basics of correct notes, rhythms, tempo, and dynamics. However, one student seemed to capture the spirit of the music and tell us through sound about a "Curious Story," and the other student was not aware or did not know how to express the emotion of the Schubert music. My theory is that one student had learned principles of musical structure and interpretation, such as shaping phrases through dynamics, articulation, and tempo, while the other student had not. I will attempt in this chapter to suggest a way of teaching that will help teachers and students make interpretative choices.

Teaching musical concepts and their expressive relationships enables students to see more similarities than differences between compositions. No longer will students start from scratch with each new piece. Concepts that students learned in previous music will transfer to music that is new to them. In order to organize one's teaching based on principles, musical and piano performance concepts are presented as the real basics of what to teach in music. I use the term "real basics of music" in a tongue-in-cheek manner since basics are usually considered to be learning the facts of note names and rhythm names rather than the musicality created by the relationships of notes and rhythms.

Conceptual learning helps students develop a thought process about music so they are not merely memorizing musical facts. This and the next chapter equip teachers with *what* to teach in music—concepts and principles. All other chapters suggest *how* to teach problem-solving skills that encourage the development of student insight into musical concepts.

Experienced pianists can make generalizations about style, melody, phrasing, harmony, key, and form. They have played extensive repertoire and studied music theory and history. However, theory and history are not often taught in the piano lesson. Instead these subjects are relegated to a classroom or computer lab. Thus, the teacher does not relate the theory and history to the piano literature being studied in lessons. It has been left to the music student to make the connections between performance, theory, and history—what the composer wrote and how it should be interpreted. More often than not, the connection is not made. It is our responsibility as piano teachers to help students make the connections.

Students not only must be taught music theory and history as related to the score but also how to expressively portray the score in their performance. Students often learn musical symbols without theoretical understanding. They are conditioned to respond correctly to notes, rhythms, legato, staccato, and dynamic signs but do not respond to the symbols expressively. They play chord changes with the same dynamic level without regard for the tension and release of the harmonic progression in the phrase.

Music touches the emotions. The musical symbols serve the higher end of communicating the composer's thoughts and emotions. For students to respond to what they play with feeling and understanding, teachers must help them make connections between symbols and interpretation.

What teaching approach will train students to be knowledgeable and sensitive in playing the piano? Jerome Bruner, a leader in educational theory, believes we should teach the structure of the subject matter or how things are related rather than merely teaching the facts and techniques (12). Bruner's theory certainly applies to teaching music. For example, learning the facts of quarter notes and letter names on the staff is secondary to understanding the structure of a melody as it ascends and descends in even or uneven rhythm patterns. Structural awareness invokes an aural and emotional response to the music. For instance, if a student is listening to even rhythm patterns of a processional as he plays, he is more likely to respond to the noble character of the music. If the student is only concerned with the fact that each quarter note gets one beat, then he probably will have no emotional reaction to the rhythm.

Teachers can guide students' interpretive and analytical choices by helping them learn general principles of music and its performance. Principles are truisms about music. The formation of a principle requires two or more musical concepts. The concept of pitch means nothing in music without the concept of rhythm. Rhythm needs structure through form to be coherent and melody needs harmony to convey tension and release. Just as bricks and mortar don't make the house, notes and rhythms don't make the song. Meter and phrasing give the melody continuity. Dynamics, tempo, and articulation portray the character of the music. The intricate relationship of all concepts is part of what makes each composition unique.

The basic elements or concepts of music will be identified individually before discussing principle formation in Chapter 5. Concepts in music can be grouped into three categories:

• Basic concepts to realize the music
• Aesthetic concepts to interpret the music
• Technique concepts to physically play the music

A simple yet global definition of pitch is that sounds can move higher or lower. Intervals and note patterns are a part of the concept of pitch. Again,

Table 4.1

Basic	Aesthetic	Technique
Pitch	Dynamics	Topography
Rhythm	Articulation	Technique—use of fingers, hands, arms
Texture	Tempo	
Scale		
Form		
Tension/release		

a simple yet global definition of the aesthetic concept of articulation is that sounds can be attached or detached. Legato, staccato, and slur are a part of the concept of articulation. The global definition of technique is that sounds are made by movement of the fingers, wrists, arms, and body. Flexible wrists, fingering, and posture are a part of the concept of technique.

The elements of music are too often taught as individual facts without regard for transfer to other music. Presenting the elements to students in a conceptual manner will allow them to apply the concept to any music. For instance, the student who learns the notes of "Hot Cross Buns" as E–D–C will not understand how to play another song that uses the notes A–G–F. However, learning that pitches move up or down or stay the same is a concept that is similar for all music. In "Hot Cross Buns," the student learns to play in a pitch range of a third, to start on the highest note, and to follow the pitch direction up and down. The student can easily transpose the tune beginning on A.

Table 4.1 is a convenient way to remember the musical concepts for easy access in teaching. I call the eleven concepts my guidebook for teaching. These concepts provide focus to each lesson. If the student is confused with one approach, try using other concepts to reach the student.

Armed with the eleven concepts in Table 4.1, the teacher has a wealth of approaches to help students understand music. Individual concepts are defined in Tables 4.2, 4.3, and 4.4, but please add your own definitions. No matter whether the student is beginning or advanced, the structure of music learned through the relation of concepts is the same—only the complexity of the concept changes. For example, the beginner may understand one aspect of texture such as pitches

Table 4.2

Basic Concepts	Examples
Pitch: Sounds can move higher or lower.	Direction, intervals, note names, clefs, staff, flats, sharps, naturals
Rhythm: Sounds can be different lengths.	Even or uneven values; note value names of quarter, half, etc.; difference between beat and rhythm; augmentation, diminution; harmonic rhythm; meter
Texture: Sounds can sound simultaneously.	Two or more notes played together, counterpoint, homophony, polyphony, ostinato, voicing, balance, triads of clusters, thirds, fourths, fifths
Scale: Sounds can be organized around pitch centers.	Major, minor, modal, twelve-tone, pentatonic, whole tone, five-finger scale
Form: Sounds can be organized.	Binary, ternary, sonata allegro, suite, measure, meter, phrase
Tension/release: Sounds progress between points of tension and repose.	Phrasing, arsis/thesis, phrase shape, harmony, V to I, triad inversions, chord progressions, tonic, dominant seventh chords

Table 4.3

Aesthetic Concepts	Examples
Dynamics: Sounds can have different strengths.	*p f mf mp ff pp*, sotto voce, voicing, dynamic accent, phrase shape, contrast
Articulation: Sounds can be attached or detached.	Legato, staccato, pedal, portato, pedaled staccato, leggiero
Tempo: Sounds can follow one another at a faster or slower pace.	Allegro, andante, vivace, ritardando, accelerando, a tempo, rubato, agogic accents

Table 4.4

Technique Concepts	Examples
Topography: The keyboard is organized by a pattern of black and white notes and a pitch range from left to right of low to high.	Fingers and wrists adjust to the varying position of black and/or white keys
Technique: Use of fingers, hands, wrists, arms, body, and feet in a coordinated manner to produce sound.	Fingering, hand position, weight transfer, posture, foot position for pedaling

sounding simultaneously, whereas the advanced student may understand a more complex aspect of texture such as homophony or polyphony.

I am deeply grateful to Guy Duckworth for introducing me to teaching and learning music conceptually. Please refer to the Bibliography for articles and books by him on the topic.

Although the preceding list is by no means complete, it does isolate the concept to its most basic form. An explanation of each concept will be given as a prelude to forming general principles about music. Certainly the explanations do not cover all aspects of the concept. I encourage you to make your own explanations of musical concepts. Keep in mind that no one concept produces music. It is the interrelationships of concepts that lead us to a deeper understanding of music.

Basic Concepts. The basic concepts of pitch, rhythm, texture, scale, form, and tension and release are the grammar of music.

Pitch is the concept that sounds can move higher or lower by stepwise motion, skips, or repeats. Of utmost importance in learning the concept of pitch is the ability to *hear* how the sound moves. Singing and listening exercises develop the ability to hear pitch direction and to discriminate between intervals. Thus, the student *hears* notes on the score in his mind before he plays, and this aural reading heightens his sensitivity to the sound. An awareness of sound is a necessity for sensitive interpretations.

Louise planned her lessons with eight-year-old Laura to make sure she understood that the notes on the staff represent sound. They sang and played the off-staff melodies from the method book, and Louise emphasized the up-and-down direction of the sound and its relationship to the piano. When she introduced the grand staff, she continued to emphasize the up-and-down direction of sound on the staff. She helped Laura realize that notes on the grand staff are labeled A–B–C–D–E–F–G, but this information was mainly useful in orienting her to where to begin on the instrument. The notation actually indicates if the motion of the sound is up, down, or the same and shows the distances between notes.

An intervallic approach to note reading uses clef signs as references for note location and emphasizes reading by direction and intervals. Intervallic reading encourages listening to the sound and feeling the interval shape in the hand. Conversely, a factual approach is reading the note names of each pitch on the staff and associating them with note names of the piano. The intervallic approach to teaching pitch is very pianistic as playing the piano is visually similar to the movement and direction of notes on the score.

I was concerned about my pedagogy students' approach to teaching the staff to a group of three eight-year-olds. For two months the children had been learning about rhythm and melodies in a conceptual manner. They played melodies by ear in all major and minor five-note scales and improvised easily to given rhythm patterns including eighth notes and dotted quarter notes. However, when the two student teachers introduced reading, they threw the conceptual

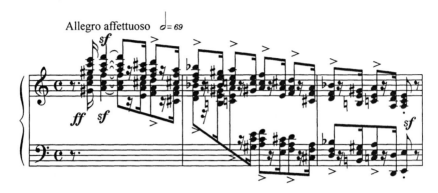

Example 4.1. Chord pattern recognition aids ease of playing in visually deceiving passages.
Robert Schumann, Piano Concerto in A Minor, Op. 54, first movement, measures 1–3 (New York: G. Schirmer, 1945).

process out the window and instead had the students point and say the letter names. The children did not understand. They had developed the habit of first clapping the rhythms and then singing the melody while listening for direction of up, down, and repeat and discriminating between steps and skips. When they were asked to name notes without the context of direction and intervals, the melody did not make sense. Is a melody just a collection of note names? No— melodies are patterns of sound that ascend and descend with expressive turns of steps and skips. The children understood this and at the next lesson the teachers reinforced note reading by saying the direction, interval, and finally the note name. The teachers directed the students to point to each note of "Away in a Manger" and say "starts on C, repeats C, steps down to B♭, steps down to A, repeats A, steps down to G, steps down to F, etc." The children then realized how the grand staff relates to the movement of melodies and the keyboard.

Recognizing pitch patterns in the score and their similarities and differences aids in understanding the compositional principles of motive, repetition, sequence, and contrast. Aspects of pitch discussed are applicable to the music studied by the advanced student as well as the beginning student. The advanced student can appreciate the intricacies of a melody by Mozart, and the beginner can delight in recognizing a repeated pattern. Uta, a high school student, had a eureka moment in her second week of reading the Schumann Concerto in A Minor (Ex. 4.1). She stumbled through the opening chords, playing four notes in the right hand and two notes in the left hand. The passage was visually deceiving to her until she recognized the chord pattern of the same three-note chord in each hand. By grouping the pitches into a pattern, she immediately changed the fingering and played the passage with ease.

Rhythm is the concept that sounds can be different lengths. The student who recognizes the character of rhythm not only perceives the note values but the emotional impact of the rhythm as well. The fact that a quarter note gets one beat and a half note two beats is less important than the feeling those note values have in time and space. Students can identify with the running movement of eighth notes, the lilting movement of $\frac{6}{8}$ meter, and the drama of long notes followed by short notes such as in the opening to Beethoven's Sonata, Op. 13 (*Pathétique*).

I am an advocate of eurhythmics, good rhythm, which is an approach to music that stresses feeling the beat and rhythm in the body. Émile Jaques-Dalcroze (1865–1950), a Swiss musician and educator who founded the Dalcroze Method, trained students in musical rhythm through body experience. Certificate training is available in Dalcroze Eurhythmics; however, a creative teacher can adapt the idea for his studio. Beginners can walk the beat and clap the rhythm while counting out loud. Advancing students will benefit by moving to the beat and rhythm and dancing the steps of a waltz, minuet, or gigue that they might be playing. Eurhythmics is an effective strategy for developing coordination. The student can tap the rhythm of both hands while counting out loud. Through a physical sensation of the written score, students develop rhythmic stability, musicality, and a sense of forward motion. Even if the teacher and student lack grace and coordination, moving will help them internalize the rhythm for a better performance.

I consider eurhythmics a "cure-all" for many student problems. By walking a steady beat while clapping and chanting the rhythms, beginners learn to distinguish between pulse and rhythm. Joyce applied eurhythmics in her lesson with Craig by having him play the rhythm of "Stomp Dance" (*Hal Leonard Student Piano Library, Piano Solos, Book 1*) on a wooden block while "stomping" the beat. Although he was uncoordinated at first, he mastered the feat in successive lessons.

With eurhythmics training, time signatures make sense because the student observes that in $\frac{4}{4}$ time he walks four beats while he claps two quarters and a half note. Students are usually so confused about why a half note is counted 3–4 at the end of a measure when it gets 1–2 beats. Walking the beats solves that problem. Movement gives students kinesthetic information in order to analyze the music they hear.

Teaching the dotted-quarter rhythm by walking the beat while clapping the quarter-dot-eighth rhythm is an excellent resource for this difficult rhythm. In Example 4.2, students match up a step on the quarter note with another step on the dot of the quarter followed by an eighth. Thus they see that two steps match the clapping of the dotted quarter and eighth rhythm.

The advanced student can learn about phrase rhythm through eurhythmics. Ask the student to conduct the beats while stepping the rhythm in order to gain an awareness of the phrase rhythm. For instance, have him notice the note values on beat one of each measure of a four-measure phrase and the rhythm of the upbeats that propel the motion to each downbeat. The coordination is difficult, but it is well worth the effort as the result is improved performance.

The advanced student can learn harmonic rhythm—the rhythmic pattern of harmonic changes. Observing that chords change every two beats, for example,

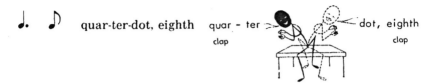

Example 4.2. Eurythmics solidifies understanding of the dotted-quarter and eighth rhythm.
Guy Duckworth, *Keyboard Explorer* (Evansville, Ill.: M-F Music, div. of Opus Music Publishers, 1980).

Example 4.3. The harmony changes every two to four beats.
Ludwig van Beethoven, Sonata, Op. 27, No. 2, first movement, measures 5–8.

assists coordination as well as interpretation of the tension and release of the chords. Mary Ann asked her high school student Marion to play "Twinkle, Twinkle, Little Star" by ear and harmonize with tonic, dominant, and subdominant chords. Marion realized that the chords are played every two beats and that the harmony changes every two beats. She applied her new knowledge of harmonic rhythm to the first movement of Beethoven's *Moonlight Sonata* (Ex. 4.3). Marion blocked the chords and observed that the harmonic changes were usually every two to four beats. She read the piece much more easily because she anticipated that the chords change every two to four beats.

Teaching rhythm in a conceptual manner as suggested in the previous examples develops a physical and emotional awareness of rhythm. The labels of rhythm—dotted quarter and eighth—are only useful for talking about note values. Rhythm must be felt in order to be understood.

Texture is the concept that sounds can occur simultaneously. Textures can be thick with chords of four or more notes or thin with as few as two parts. Aspects of texture that are a concern for performers are the balance of predominant and subordinate parts and the coordination of playing more than one part at a time. These two aspects of the concept of texture prevail through all levels of advancement. Beginners learn that a melody is projected above a chordal accompaniment. Intermediate students learn to voice chords within the hand so that one note is projected above the others. My student Karl was playing Aram

Khachaturian's "Ivan Sings" and had mastered playing the melody more loudly than the chordal accompaniment. However, when he followed the dynamics for the right-hand melody, his left hand got louder, too, and he ended up covering the melody with the accompaniment. Learning to shape a complex texture requires the coordination of playing the right-hand melody louder than the left-hand chords, plus the subtle phrasing of the chords in conjunction with the more exaggerated melodic phrasing.

Textures may be homophonic or polyphonic. Beginners understand polyphonic counterpoint as the left hand imitating the right hand, and advanced students play a fugue with emphasis on each entry of the subject. Contemporary chords—clusters and chords of fourths and fifths—can be understood more easily with a conceptual approach to texture. All are a part of sounds occurring simultaneously.

Scale is a sequence of sounds in ascending or descending order and can be organized around different pitch centers. This definition allows for the myriad of scale types, not only major and minor, but also modal, blues, pentatonic, whole tone, and synthetic scales. Atonal music is the absence of tonal center and twelve-tone music serializes each of the twelve notes of the octave. My point in listing these scales is to acknowledge that sounds can be organized in many different ways. However, I will refrain from explaining each of the scale types.

While students develop their technical facility by practicing major and minor scales, teachers also can help them understand that every composition is based on a scale. By identifying the key signature and tonal center, students limit their note choices to the seven notes in the major or minor scale, instead of all twelve notes in the octave. Thus, the odds are better that the student plays correctly the first time.

Most scale constructions have a sense of tension and release. The leading tone is a strong pull to the tonic in major and minor scales. The lowered second scale degree pulls to the tonic in the Phrygian scale (E–F–G–A–B–C–D–E). The lowered seventh softens the tension in resolving to the tonic in the mixolydian scale (G–A–B–C–D–E–F–G). In the whole-tone scale, it is unclear what note leads to what, since all steps are whole steps.

Too often, major and minor are the only scales taught, which excludes many beautiful possibilities. Students further limit themselves by identifying every key signature as major, even if it is in minor. Carefully analyzing each piece by naming the last note of the piece as the tonic and observing recurring accidentals in both melody and accompaniment will enable the student to develop good habits of verifying the key signature.

Modal scales give us another myriad of sound possibilities, as seen in Example 4.4. Each mode has a unique sound that is easily understood by observing the differences between the major and minor scales. For instance, Lydian is just like the major scale except the fourth note is raised a half step. Dorian is just like the natural minor scale except the sixth note is raised a half step. Students who learn modal scales discover that scales are a succession of whole steps and two half steps that occur in various places. Thus, they gain a conceptual understanding

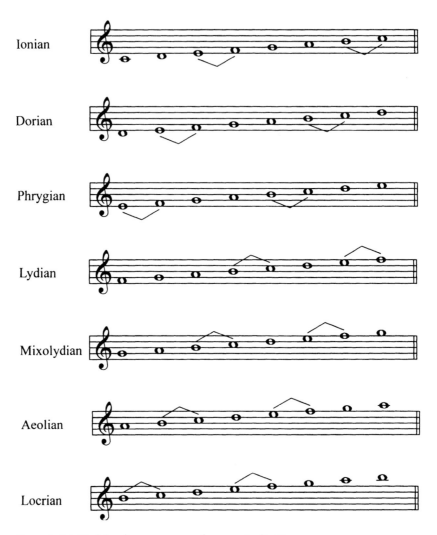

Ionian

Dorian

Phrygian

Lydian

Mixolydian

Aeolian

Locrian

Example 4.4. Modal scales encourage scale conceptualization.

of scale structures. The study of scales in piano lessons can be an enlightening experience about the many possibilities of scale organizations.

Form is the concept that sounds can be organized. Binary, ternary, sonata, and other structural forms are included in the concept of form. However, a basic unit of form is a single measure or motive, followed by a phrase of several measures. Meter is the organization of sounds into measures of duple, triple, or asymmetrical time.

Children can move to the flow of a nursery rhyme to hear meter and phrase. For instance, by swinging the arms on the naturally stressed words in the song "Happy Birthday," as underlined in Example 4.5, the child naturally feels the

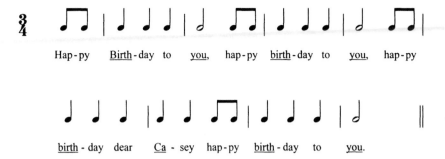

Hap-py Birth-day to you, hap-py birth-day to you, hap-py

birth-day dear Ca-sey hap-py birth-day to you.

Example 4.5. Identify meter by observing the naturally stressed words in "Happy Birthday."

$\frac{3}{4}$ meter. The stressed words—birth-you-birth-you-birth-Casey-birth-you—coincide with the first beat of each of the measures in this eight-measure phrase. Thus students learn the natural flow of music in phrases and its organization into strong and weak stress.

Repetition and contrast can be taught in an eight-measure melody as well as in the larger binary or sonata forms. For instance, in "Happy Birthday" students observe that the repeated eighths are an upbeat to each two-measure phrase; and that a large skip is an upbeat to the second measure of the first two phrases. The building of tension through contrast in the last two phrases is seen in the octave skip to the first beat in measure 5 and the repeated C changing to B flat as an upbeat to the penultimate measure.

Students studying a sonata learn to expect two contrasting themes in the exposition, a development of the themes, and a return to the two themes both in the tonic key. Aleatoric music, with a lack of scale and harmony clues, may best be understood through form by observing recurrent pitch and rhythm patterns and contrast of moods. Analyzing form illuminates pitch, rhythm, and harmonic patterns in the music, all of which contribute to expressive interpretations.

Tension and release is the concept that sounds move in and out of states of tension and release. Learning harmony as an aspect of the concept of tension and release will help students react emotionally to their analysis and performance of chord progressions. Students learn to understand that the dominant chord has more emotional tension than the tonic chord that releases that tension.

Phrasing is also an aspect of tension and release. Learning to phrase so that the music has a sense of forward motion is an important interpretive goal. The ebb and flow of the music is an emotional response. If the performer does not move between states of tension and release, the playing is colorless. The delight and joy we receive from music may be due to the emotion projected through states of tension and release in the music.

Tension and release is projected in part through contrasting dynamics. Students need to learn the basics of dynamic phrasing as the dynamic markings for

Example 4.6. Shape a phrase through metrical understanding.
Frédéric Chopin, Prelude in B Minor, Op. 28, No. 6, measures 1–4. From *Encore*, Book 1, ed. Jane Magrath (Van Nuys, Calif.: Alfred Publishing Co., 1990).

phrasing are not often written in the score. Following are guidelines for dynamic stress as it relates to the metrical organization.

- No two successive notes are played the same strength because of their metrical relationship in the measure.
- The first beat of the measure is stressed with secondary stress on the third beat in $\frac{4}{4}$ meter.
- Just as the upbeat of the conductor's baton visually gives the preparation for the downbeat, a student's performance must have tension on the upbeats to arrive at repose on the downbeats. Shape the phrase dynamically toward the downbeat by playing a crescendo on the upbeats 2 3 4, the arsis, and release on beat 1, the thesis.
- Metrical organization also extends to the four-measure phrase with the first and third measures being arrival points. The second measure leads to the climactic third measure and the fourth measure softens with the release of tension. In Example 4.6, Frédéric Chopin indicates dynamic shaping in the Prelude in B Minor, Op. 28, No. 6.

Aesthetic Concepts. The aesthetic concepts of dynamics, articulation, and tempo are the tools for expressing music.

Dynamics is the concept that sounds have different strengths. Beginning students learn to hear contrasting sounds of soft and loud and to physically distinguish between them at the piano. Soon they learn more subtle shading of crescendo and diminuendo. An advanced awareness of the concept of dynamics is the ability to hear between the notes played. The pianist has the difficult task of creating the illusion that a crescendo continues through several notes, even though the piano sound immediately softens when the key is struck. The ability to hear from sound to sound is most important in developing a student's musicianship. Technique goes hand in hand with dynamic control so the student learns to make a beautiful soft sound as well as a resonant loud sound.

Students can learn to control dynamics to portray the meaning of the music

Example 4.7. Crescendo to the upper note to heighten the melodic tension of the octave and seventh.
Daniel Gottlieb Türk, "Gefühl der Wehmuth," measures 5–8. From *Leichte Klavierstücke: Band I* (München: G. Henle Verlag, 1977).

Example 4.8. Forte dynamics, articulate sixteenths, and a lively tempo suggest the image of horns announcing a hunt.
Daniel Gottlieb Türk, "Die Waldhörner und das Echo," measures 6–10. From *Leichte Klavierstücke: Band I* (München: G. Henle Verlag, 1977).

by reacting to pitch and rhythm clues. Following are a few guidelines to illustrate how students can interpret the composer's note and rhythm indications.

- Crescendo when notes ascend, decrescendo when notes descend (Ex. 4.6).
- Stress the upper note in a melodic leap to create tension and soften the stepwise resolution (Ex. 4.7).
- Select a tempo, dynamic level, and articulation that will project the mood. Dotted rhythms in the "Hunting Song" by Daniel Gottlieb Türk (Ex. 4.8) suggest the blare of the horns to announce a fox hunt, a European sport. A lively tempo and energetic articulation of the sixteenths help create the image of a hunt.

Encourage students to make imaginative associations of moods and stories to go with the music they play. The image will help them phrase the music to project the meaning they feel. Visual images might be a loud violent thunderstorm or a soft delicate rain. Emotional associations might be raging anger or gentle love. Rather than merely giving information that piano is soft and forte is loud, teach students to become sensitive to the context of dynamic markings.

Articulation is the concept that sounds can be detached or attached. Touches

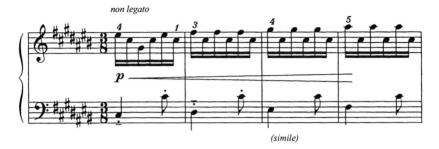

Example 4.9. Use non-legato articulation in Baroque music.
Johann Sebastian Bach, Prelude in C Sharp Major, BWV 848, measures 1–4. From *The Well-Tempered Clavier*, vol. I, ed. Willard A. Palmer (Sherman Oaks, Calif.: Alfred Publishing Co., 1981).

range from the shortest staccato to the most connected finger legato. Articulation includes the sustaining quality of the damper and sostenuto pedals as well as the accent pedal to emphasize particular notes or chords. The length of a staccato can be very short or slightly disconnected. Knowledge of the performance practice of the style period will enable the student to make decisions about the composer's intentions. Following are examples of articulation in selected passages of music by Bach, Brahms, and Bartók.

1) Because Johann Sebastian Bach gave no indications for articulation, advise students to play detached to capture the plucked sound of the harpsichord. Play non-legato and staccato throughout the Bach Prelude in C sharp major as marked by editor Maurice Hinson (Ex. 4.9). Also utilize the slur and staccato capabilities of the piano to articulate the counterpoint of each voice of a fugue and capture the dance quality of the bourrée, sarabande, minuet, and gigue.

2) Johannes Brahms often marked staccato with a slur over the notes while using legato pedal. The Romantic composers did not mark pedaling except when it might be out of the ordinary, but the pedal is nearly always used to enhance the color of the wide pitch range and harmonic changes in this period. Through his markings, Brahms gave us aesthetic directions for the tone quality as seen in his Rhapsody in G Minor (Ex. 4.10).

3) Béla Bartók marked very definite types of detachment of slur, staccato, tenuto, and various accent marks as related to articulation (Ex. 4.11).

Pedaling is an important concept in teaching articulation. Students learn timing of when to press and lift the pedal. Karl, a student of mine, mistakenly pedaled on the syncopated chords rather than on main beats in Khachaturian's "Ivan Sings" (Ex. 4.12). He lost the melody sound in the right hand. When he changed the pedal on beat one, he heard the melody and harmony. Karl had to learn to coordinate his foot movement with hearing the melody and harmony.

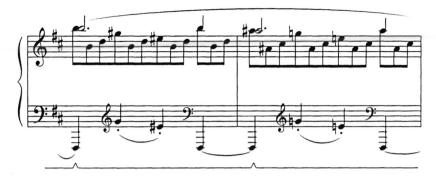

Example 4.10. In Brahms's music, the staccatos with pedal have a bell-like tone quality. Johannes Brahms, Rhapsody in G Minor, Op. 79, No. 2, measures 46–47. From *At the Piano with Brahms,* ed. Maurice Hinson (Van Nuys, Calif.: Alfred Publishing Co., 1988).

Example 4.11. Bartók indicates lengths of staccatos and strengths of accents. Béla Bartók, "Bear Dance," measures 5–8. From *Masters of the Early Contemporary Period,* ed. Maurice Hinson (Van Nuys, Calif.: Alfred Publishing Co., 1992).

Example 4.12. Pedal on main beats to catch the melody notes in the pedal. Aram Khachaturian, "Ivan Sings," measures 18–19. From *Alfred's Group Piano for Adults,* Book 2, ed. E. L. Lancaster and Kenon D. Renfrow (Van Nuys, Calif.: Alfred Publishing Co., 1996).

Tempo is the concept that sounds can move at different paces. Insisting that students play in a steady pulse is paramount to musical development. Without a consistent pulse the energy of the rhythm and the beauty of the melody cannot be heard and felt. Students get excited about playing when they hear the flow of the music. Students must not only know what a time signature means but also must learn to internalize the pulse. Please refer to the eurhythmics suggestions in the rhythm discussion for ways to develop an internal feeling for pulse.

Perhaps no other concept can affect mood more than the tempo chosen. Students should be encouraged to use their imaginations to decide a mood and let the tempo selected be a natural portrayal of that mood. Mindy, a high school student, chose the moods for each section of the Chopin Ballade, Op. 52, No. 4. She said that using her imagination gave her more freedom to express the music. It also helped her play with more tempo consistency. Previously, she used so much rubato that phrases did not have forward motion and the music lacked purpose.

Rubato, the flexibility of tempo for expressiveness, is part of the concept of tempo. I was amazed at the difference in the performance of one of my students of Chopin's Prelude in B Minor from one week to the next. Lela played beautifully the second week. However, the week before her playing was mechanical, shapeless, and inaccurate. At that lesson we talked about a cello analogy for a rich sounding left-hand melody, analyzed chords to correct missed notes, and experimented with rubato playing. I was amazed at how she changed the piece in a week. She felt the music for the first time because of her expressive rubato. Through identifying emotionally with the music, she heard and projected the left-hand melody and was motivated to correct the chords. Her expressive playing contributed to ease in playing accurately.

Technique Concepts. The concepts of topography and technique are the means for playing the music.

The student may play very musically but if the technique is weak, the music portrayed will have less of an impact. Problems with both aesthetic and basic concepts, such as lack of precision and inconsistent dynamic control, are directly related to lack of technical proficiency.

Technique is the concept of using the fingers, wrists, arms, and body to play the piano. More has been written about technique in piano pedagogy than any other subject, perhaps rightly so, because good playing is impossible without good technique. Certainly the importance of technique should be kept in the proper context: technique is the means to the end of an artistic performance. Sensitivity to the musical import of a composition is the motivation for good technique.

Perhaps there are more diverse opinions about piano technique than any other topic. *A Symposium for Pianists and Teachers: Strategies to Develop the Mind and Body for Optimal Performance* (2002) is among the many sources that offer diverse opinions about healthy technique and movement.

Start from the first lesson to develop good posture, strong finger joints, and relaxed arms and hands in order to transfer the weight from finger to finger. Posture is vital to this development. The pianist should adopt the dancer's posture of hips tucked under, neck and spine in line, rib cage pulled up from the pelvis, and feet parallel on the floor.

The height of the bench should allow the upper arms to relax from the shoulders and the lower arms and wrists to be level with the keyboard while playing. Do whatever it takes to attend to good posture. The young student is often more comfortable standing if the bench is an inappropriate height. Provide books for the student to sit on in order to raise the position or try a chair to lower the position.

Inquire about the height of the student's practice bench or chair and inform the parents to make sure the "adapted" bench is in place for practice sessions. A sitting position that is too high with the arms reaching down to the keyboard or too low with the arms reaching up to the keyboard will interrupt the natural release of weight into the keys. The goal is to avoid unnecessary tension in any part of the playing mechanism. With repetitive motions causing conditions such as carpal tunnel syndrome, posture cannot be overlooked.

To transfer the weight from finger to finger, release the weight only in the fingers playing and relax the other fingers. Unnecessary tension is often seen when the pinkie or other fingers pop up. In a relaxed and balanced hand the wrist adjusts position to support each finger, as seen in lateral wrist movement to the right in ascending passages and wrist movement to the left in descending passages. In other words, the hand, wrist, and arm move as a coordinated unit in the direction of the notes.

Control of *pianissimo* to *fortissimo* dynamics is achieved by releasing lighter weight of the finger for *piano*, then the weight of the hand for *mezzopiano*, the weight of the lower arm for *mezzoforte*, and heavier weight from the upper arm and back for *forte*. With a well-coordinated technique, the pianist is capable of the softest *pianissimo* and the most resonant *fortissimo*.

Practicing exercises is important to develop control of hand position, dynamics, and articulation. I rarely use prepared exercises such as Hanon and Czerny because I prefer to use major, minor, and double-third modal five-finger patterns; major and minor scales played in octaves as well as single notes; and major, minor, and diminished seventh arpeggios. Certainly Hanon and other exercises transposed to all keys could serve similar ends. Also excellent music—as well as technical etudes—are studies written by Johann Burgmüller, Stephen Heller, Moritz Moszkowski, and Frédéric Chopin. Also good are studies by twentieth-century pedagogical composers such as Robert Vandall and Catherine Rollin, and etude editions by Jane Magrath and Keith Snell.

Developing a good technique is only a means to an end. Students must hear how they want the music to go. They must hear a melody to be able to physically project it. In fact, focusing on the musical aspects often solves the technical problem. That was the case in a technique problem that Mary Ann's high school student, Marion, was having in Sonata in D Major by Mateo Albéniz. She had physical tension in a pattern of repeated harmonic sixths and also had trouble

Example 4.13. Physical tension is lessened by legato fingering for the melody.
Mateo Albéniz, Sonata in D Major, measures 16–24. From *Masterpieces with Flair!*
Book 3, ed. Jane Magrath (Van Nuys, Calif.: Alfred Publishing Co., 1993).

with melodic movement in the sixths (Ex. 4.13). After Mary Ann had the pupil listen for the melody line in the repeated chords, she voiced the sixth so that the melody was projected and the lower note of the sixth was softened. Singing the top note of the sixths as a melody made her realize that fingering needed to be changed from 5–5–5 to 5–4–4 for continuity in the melody. Hearing the melody released the physical tension she felt in playing the repeated sixths.

Topography is the concept of the geography of the piano: the organization of the black and white keys into patterns and a pitch range from left to right of low to high. The groups of two and three black keys are guides to the pianist to see and feel the keyboard. The topography directly affects fingering choices with the longer fingers of 2–3–4 more comfortable on the higher-level black keys and the thumbs naturally placed on the lower white keys. Consider the following scale fingering.

1) Cross the hand over the thumb when approaching a black key.
2) Pass the thumb under the hand after a black key.

These two points make scale fingering very efficient because the shorter distance from the white to the black key requires less hand movement as opposed to a white-to-white key cross or pass. The composer or editor often marks scale fingering in this manner in the music. As can be seen in Example 4.14, the traditional major scale fingering will change for the left hand if this fingering principle is used.

In a good hand position the hand arches like one is holding a miniature football. The fingers drop from the knuckles, the pinkie straightens to act like a long finger, and the thumb perches on its edge to cradle the ball. This shape is very natural when playing five-finger patterns beginning on black notes. But beware of C and G positions, which take extra effort to shape the hand. If students lack a good hand shape, teach the D flat and A flat five-finger scales (pentachord) rather than the keys of C and G.

An excellent exercise to train the hand to adjust to the various topographies is one built on modal pentachords. In Example 4.15, notice that only one note

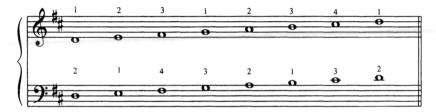

Example 4.14. Choose scale fingering related to keyboard topography. The thumb is before a black key in a cross-over and is after the black key in a pass-under.

Example 4.15. Modal pentachords develop hand position.

changes for each pentachord. Playing the exercise in double thirds further develops finger independence and builds strength.

Summary of concepts. Concepts in themselves mean nothing in music until they are related to one another to form musical principles. The pianist's ability to interrelate the basic, aesthetic, and technique concepts is what produces a performance of beautiful music. Most teachers would say one of their goals is to teach themselves out of a job. Teachers want students to think on their own so that their practice is productive and their progress is consistent. Equipping students with conceptual knowledge is a way to help them make their own decisions about music performance and interpretation. Our task is to guide students to observe conceptual relationships and how they are similar in all music, and assist them in appreciating the differences when a composer breaks from the norm.

Suggested Reading

Anderson, "Skip the Opening Lecture and Play."
Andre and Phye, eds., *Cognitive Classroom Learning.*
Bernstein, *With Your Own Two Hands.*
Caldwell, *Expressive Singing: Dalcroze Eurhythmics for Voice.*
Camp, *Developing Piano Performance.*
Coats, *A Correlational Study of Aesthetic Piano Performance and a Learning Approach Based on a Gestalt Theory of Problem Solving.*
——, "Count and Move Out Loud."
——, "Dancing the Baroque Dance Suites."
——, et al., eds., "The Heart of the Matter: Rhythm."
Duckworth, *Keyboard Musician,* Book VI: *The Symmetrical Keyboard.*
——, "Fingering Logic."
——, "Keyboard Literacy."
——, "What Are We Teaching—Concepts or Details?"
Jaques-Dalcroze, *Rhythm, Music, and Education.*
Kropff, ed., *A Symposium for Pianists and Teachers.*
Schnebly-Black and Moore, *Rhythm: One on One.*
Serafine, *Music as Cognition.*
Shockley, *Mapping Music: For Faster Learning and Secure Memory.*

Further Thought

- List the musical concepts. Describe their global properties.
- What is eurhythmics? What movement activities could you do in each lesson?
- What is conceptual teaching? Give an example.
- How can conceptualizing motivate students?

5 The Real Basics of Music: Musical Principles

As teachers we tend to leave out a step in the lesson before we send the student home to practice. We get them to play well in the lesson through modeling or verbal instruction, yet we don't review what they learned and how. If we leave out this step, they will practice by copying what sound they heard in the lesson, but will not know how they got there. By identifying general principles about how and why they were able to play so beautifully, students begin to trust that they can apply principles to similar problems they have in their practice. The road to independent thinking is in part a process of becoming aware of musical problems, and then trusting one's intuition to apply general principles learned in lessons to practicing alone.

> *Principle Formation. Principles are generalizations that could apply to all music and all levels of advancement.*

Two or more musical concepts form a general principle. For instance, when pitches look higher on the score, they sound higher on the piano. The concept of pitch direction coupled with the topography of the piano forms this principle. *When pitches look higher, they sound higher* is a principle applicable to all music. The transfer potential is the value of such a principle. Training students to think about the global properties of music will ensure that they really understand concepts and can transfer what they have learned. Following are examples of principles of pitch, phrasing, and key, with the concepts listed in parentheses. The examples are suggestions for encouraging the reader to make other and perhaps more significant global ideas applicable to his or her teaching.

- In stepwise motion, adjacent fingers are played (pitch and technique).
- Longer note values end phrases (rhythm and form).
- Shorter note values often occur in the third measure of a phrase (rhythm and form).
- The final note of a melody is the tonic of the key (form and scale).
- The first phrase often ends on the dominant chord and leads to the second phrase ending on the tonic chord (harmony, phrasing, and form).

Articulation Principle. Principles may be more specific. In Baroque music, articulation of constant eighth and sixteenth rhythms is generally detached in order to imitate the plucking mechanism of the harpsichord (articulation and rhythm). This principle applies to much of J. S. Bach's music. However, it would

Example 5.1. Bourrée principles of articulation, meter, rhythm, and form.
Johann Sebastian Bach, Bourrée in B Minor, BWV 831, measures 1–4. From *Celebration Series*, 2nd ed. Piano Repertoire Album 6 (Missisauga, Ontario: The Frederick Harris Music Co., 1994).

not be applicable to the music of Chopin, because he lived in a different century and used the sustaining capabilities of the piano.

Although Bach did not indicate articulation in the score, movements from Bach's dance suites—including minuet, sarabande, bourrée, courante, and gavotte —have varied articulations of slur, staccato, and legato. A principle relating to the bourrée is that the dance quality is captured by slurring the eighth notes and detaching the quarter notes (articulation, rhythm) (Ex. 5.1). Although the author added staccatos to this excerpt, the editor of the edition notes that the quarters may be played detached. Each dance form has its own characteristics. For instance, in Example 5.1 the bourrée is in cut time with a pickup to each four-measure phrase (meter, rhythm, form). Although the preceding principles are specific to the Baroque period, dance forms have continued to be written throughout music history (see the appendixes for Baroque and Romantic dance steps and characteristics).

Tonality Principle. If we help students find similarities in music, then the differences will have more meaning. The beginning student learns that each piece is built on a scale, which is a similarity of all beginning music. When an accidental occurs in the score, help the student feel the tension of a key change, which is most likely to the dominant key. The student can delight in the exception to the rule rather than worry about an accidental to correct. The advancing student learns that in sonata allegro form the first theme is in the tonic key and the second theme is usually in the dominant key; if the first theme is in a minor key, the second theme is usually in the relative major key. Megan, a sixteen-year-old student, and I delighted in the discovery that Beethoven did not follow the standard form and surprised us with the key he used in the second theme of the first movement of the Sonata, Op. 13. The dark introduction in C minor gives way to the impetuous allegro in C minor. Then he modulates not to the relative E flat major but to the parallel E flat minor for the second theme, which gives the theme an air of mystery. Megan, who loves the sonata, had studied sonatinas and a few sonatas, so she was aware of the similarities in classical so-

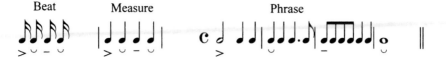

Beat	Measure	Phrase

Example 5.2. Accent structure of a beat, measure, and phrase.

natas. Megan's sensitive performance of the "Pathétique" reflects her understanding of Beethoven's departure from the norm.

Phrasing Principles. As students progress, they learn to play musically by following general principles about phrasing. Beginning students learn to shape a phrase by applying this principle: when notes go up, crescendo, when notes go down, decrescendo (pitch direction, dynamics). The advanced student has more guidelines about shaping a phrase because she knows the general structure of a four-measure phrase. The tension point of a phrase usually occurs in the third measure. To hear the tension, crescendo in the first and second measures and then resolve the tension with a diminuendo in the fourth measure of the phrase (tension/release, dynamics, form).

Students can learn a hierarchy of how to stress notes in a phrase by following these three simple interpretative concepts (Ex. 5.2).

1) Accent structure of one beat of sixteenth notes: first note has the most stress, third note less stress, and other notes softer.
2) Accent structure of a measure in common time: first note has the most stress, third note less stress, and other notes softer.
3) Accent structure of a four-measure phrase: first measure has the most stress, third measure less stress, and other measures softer (stress, form, rhythm).

However, performing with this constant accent structure is quite mechanical, even though these are basic principles of stress related to form. Also to be understood is the principle of arsis and thesis. The first beat (thesis) of the measure is stressed as a result of its preparation (arsis). The phrase builds in volume and leads to the first beat of the measure so that it is not actually played louder, but because of the crescendo before it, the first beat sounds stressed. The thesis can be the first beat of a measure as well as the first beat in the hierarchy of a phrase. My precocious sixth-grade student, Karl, said he wanted to work on dynamics— the ones not written in the score—in "Ivan Sings" from the *Adventures of Ivan* by Aram Khachaturian (Ex. 5.3). We looked at the four-measure phrases and observed the similar rhythm patterns. We talked about how the rhythm began with longer note values, became more rhythmically active in the third measure, and ended the phrase with a long note in the fourth measure. I suggested that he observe the piano marking, but crescendo to the first beat of the third measure and slightly decrescendo to the fourth measure, thus applying the principle of arsis and thesis. He played the melody only but made no difference in dy-

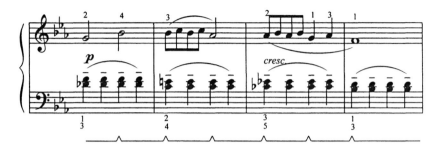

Example 5.3: Shaping a phrase dynamically in "Ivan Sings" by Aram Khachaturian.
Aram Khachaturian, "Ivan Sings," measures 10–13. From *Alfred's Group Piano for Adults,* Book 2, ed. E. L. Lancaster and Kenon D. Renfrow (Van Nuys, Calif.: Alfred Publishing Co., 1996).

namics so I asked him to exaggerate. His exaggerated dynamics made a perfectly shaped melodic phrase. Karl's perception of how loud or soft he could play was changed so he had a larger palette of sound to interpret the dynamics that were not notated.

In summary, advanced students can be expected to prepare not only a correct reading of the visual score of pitch, rhythm, and dynamics of assigned repertoire but also to apply the phrasing not notated. The beginner can learn dynamic shaping related to pitch direction and form. The same concepts are applicable for all levels of study, but the principles become more complex as the student advances.

Transfer. If musical concepts are compared between the compositions being played, then students will understand how the discussed topics relate to all music. Moving from the specific to the general helps students realize that what is learned in one piece is true for all pieces. In the following three lessons, teachers helped students see how concepts relate to all music played. Mary Ann's lesson with Caitlin focused on loud and soft, my lesson with Karl stressed playing without arm tension, and Diane planned a lesson on metrical continuity for Wes.

Dynamics Transfer. Mary Ann, a piano pedagogy graduate student, said she has improved in transferring concepts from one piece to another in her teaching. Mary Ann's lesson plan for Caitlin, a seven-year-old student, focused on understanding *forte* and *piano.* I had suggested that she help Caitlin remember *piano* and *forte* symbols by focusing on the concept of dynamics in each piece she taught. Mary Ann used the *Hal Leonard Student Piano Library, Book 1* of Lessons, Solos, and Theory. She had Caitlin play "Under Sea Voyage" softly and "Taxi Tangle" loudly in the lesson book. Then she reinforced the dynamic concepts by having Caitlin play from the solo book "Quiet Night" softly and "Bear Dance" loudly. Caitlin also had prepared the theory book assignment, which stressed *piano* and *forte.*

Mary Ann wrote in her evaluation of the lesson that as a teacher she kept a better focus on the concept to be learned than she had in previous lessons, but she felt uncomfortable that she hadn't talked about correct notes. A common concern for teachers regarding conceptual teaching is the worry that mistakes won't get corrected. However, at later lessons Caitlin was always attentive to dynamics, so she became able to focus on note reading. Mary Ann is teaching in such a way that dynamics become second nature to the beginning student. She used the method books to assist her in teaching *piano* and *forte,* and the materials were quite helpful as the dynamic concept was a focus of several pieces at the appropriate playing level for Caitlin. However, please take note of this important point: she did not rely on the books to make her lesson plan. Rather, her lesson focus was based on concepts.

Technique Transfer. To develop technical facility and ease, I give advanced students exercises to focus on hand position, finger control, and wrist, arm, and shoulder relaxation. Karl, a seventh grader, had trouble playing technical exercises with ease. He pressed his arms to his sides and used only his fingers to play. We worked on releasing the tension in his shoulders and arms, and as a result, he played with a better sound. During the same lesson, however, he played the Albert Pieczonka "Tarantella" with his arms pressed to his sides. He could not increase the tempo because of his tense, rather uncoordinated manner of playing. He released the tension in his arms as he had in the exercises and found he could play faster with ease. At the next lesson, Karl commented that during his practice he kept checking to see if his arms were tense. What a breakthrough for him to become aware of his physical tension. Karl understands a principle about technique and sound that he will continue to use in his practice.

Continuity Transfer. Diane, a graduate teaching assistant, set out to help her adult student, Wes, improve the continuity in his playing by stressing metrical accents in scales and transferring metrical stress to repertoire. Diane attempted to improve his sense of a steady pulse by having him play scales in $\frac{4}{4}$ meter—one octave of quarter notes, two octaves of eighth notes, three octaves of triplets, and four octaves of sixteenth notes. She stressed pulse, a manageable tempo, and the accent structure of the four beats. A small crescendo to each beat one seemed to propel each note to progress to the next. Later in the lesson, Wes had difficulty with continuity in the second movement of Beethoven's Sonata, Op. 13. Diane thought that as counting in $\frac{4}{4}$ meter had helped Wes's sense of pulse in the scales, counting would provide direction and continuity of pulse in the Sonata. However, Wes was having trouble with fingering because playing melody and accompaniment in one hand was new to him. Additionally, he was not using pedal, which would have helped the continuity. As Diane's supervising teacher, I suggested that she help him with the fingering of the first phrase rather than the more complex concept of phrasing, which improved the continuity.

All eleven concepts are available to us to help in solving a particular problem. If one approach does not work, another concept might. In this lesson in which continuity was the problem, counting did not help, but choosing fingering did.

Advantages of Teaching Principles. The point of teaching the structure of music through general principles is to empower students to learn on their own.

According to Jerome Bruner, students who learn underlying principles of a subject have demonstrated the following:

1. New concepts are more comprehensible to them.
2. Their memory is better because details are learned in context.
3. Their understanding is transferred to other subject matter.
4. The gap is narrowed between simple and complex knowledge. (21)

Bruner's four points for teaching general principles are demonstrated in the following illustrations.

Comprehension. Students who have direct experience with a new concept remember better than students who merely memorize the facts. For example, in a piano class devoted to learning the seven modes, students who sang each mode remembered the alterations from major or minor, whereas students who merely memorized the alterations forgot them quickly. Musical concepts are more comprehensible to students when they experience them in context such as singing a melody, moving to a rhythm, or playing a scale in the key of a composition.

Conceptual Memory. As an illustration of improved memory from learning details in their structural context, I offer a conceptual approach to memorizing. After working on conceptual memory for a few weeks, transfer students tell me that they feel secure with their memory for the first time in their study. They observe patterns in the score and are secure with the details because they have thoroughly analyzed the music conceptually. No longer do they rely only on motor memory, because aural and analytic memories are equally strong.

In teaching conceptual memory I guide students through a process from recognizing the whole to delineating the parts. The process uses improvisation at each of four steps. The score, read away from the piano, guides the student through the four stages.

Conceptual Improvisation-Memorization

1. Feel the mood
2. Intuit the formal structure and rhythmic patterns
3. Sense the pitch motion
4. Think the note patterns

This top-down approach recognizes that a musical performance is dependent on the performer's preparation in integrating three factors: (1) sensitivity to musical meaning, (2) sensitivity to musical form and style, and (3) technical skill to project musical meaning and form.

First, the student is asked to decide the mood after studying the score. I assure the student that the mood could change after getting to know the score better. Then the student improvises music *feeling* the suggested mood at the tempo indicated. We often improvise together at two pianos to lessen inhibitions about unstructured improvisation.

The second step is to look at the composition's formal structure and rhythmic patterns. Often the student claps or steps to rhythmic patterns. After the form is determined, the student improvises using the rhythmic patterns and overall form of the piece. Of course, the playing at this stage is very crude and does not require knowledge of the key or notes. The point is to study the whole piece and *intuitively* maintain the mood in the improvisation.

In the third step, the student studies key relationships, pitch motion, and patterns in order to improvise within the key, playing similar melodic and textural patterns. Emphasis is on a physical *sensation* of the music by identifying similarities and maintaining the mood.

At successive lessons, the fourth step, students look at details of the relationships of notes, rhythms, articulations, and dynamics in order to play accurately by memory. With shorter pieces the entire improvisation-memorization process can be completed in one lesson. With longer compositions the initial three steps are accomplished in one lesson; then the thinking out of details may take several days and weeks of playing both with the score and away from the score.

My experience with the process is that students become engaged immediately in the musical meaning of the piece and are much more aware of form and style. As a result, technical problems are lessened and worked out in relation to musical meaning. As Bruner says, details are learned in context.

Transfer to Musical Skills. Students who learn principles of music are able to transfer information to new music and skills. A student studying harmony observes that the progression dominant to tonic occurs at phrase endings. He transfers the principle to melodies played by ear and to memorized literature.

The solutions chosen to solve a problem should be generalizations about the concept that can be transferred to similar yet different situations.

Students will remember and use what they have learned if they understand what they have done. Some students can mimic the teacher's or other students' playing and not realize how they were able to shape a phrase or project a melody beautifully. In this situation, check their understanding by challenging the student to analyze the phrasing and transfer what they did to another composition. In the problem of identifying intervals of a melody, have the student transpose the melody to a different key using the same intervals or sing a melody by ear and name the intervals. The student's success in transferring the concept will signal that they understand how to use the concept and will ensure that the idea will be used in practice.

Complexity. The gap between simple and complex knowledge of music narrows when students understand the structure of music. This becomes evident to me during performance classes in my studio. At times the ages range from eight to eighteen and the length of study is from one to ten years. All students critique concepts such as dynamics, mood, and continuity. Young students often comment on the presence or absence of loud and soft in the playing, whereas older students elaborate on dynamic contrast and musical phrasing. The younger students express a simple understanding of volume and their older classmates model more complex knowledge of the concept.

These examples illustrate that when students learn the structure and underlying principles of music (1) new concepts are more comprehensible to them,

(2) they remember better, (3) they are able to transfer what they learn to other music, and (4) their understanding of musical concepts narrows the gap between simple and complex knowledge.

Further Thought

- Make some generalizations/principles about music.
- Give examples of conceptual transfers.
- How can transposing improve sight reading?
- How can harmonizing a melody improve memorization?

6   Designing a Curriculum

Rather than listing what music to teach, this chapter gives suggestions of how to design a curriculum by organizing the music taught. Teachers and students are fortunate to live in a time when an abundance of educational music has been written to entice students to study piano. Many beginning methods have been written in the last twenty years and are reviewed in the pedagogy texts *The Well-Tempered Keyboard Teacher* by Marienne Uszler et al. and *Practical Piano Pedagogy* by Martha Baker-Jordan. Jane Magrath has given us a valuable resource in *The Pianist's Guide to Standard Teaching and Performance Literature,* which lists intermediate repertoire by level and enables teachers to judge the difficulty of a composition on a scale from one to ten. Cathy Albergo and Reid Alexander's *Intermediate Piano Repertoire* is also a valuable resource. Maurice Hinson has compiled several volumes of the advanced piano repertoire with helpful annotations about each composition. Now let's turn to how to organize the music available for teaching.

What then is a curriculum? A curriculum is an organization of the study of music in order to guide a student to ever-increasing levels of understanding about the structure of music. Bruner says, "The task of teaching a subject to a child at any particular age is one of representing the structure of that subject in terms of the child's way of viewing things." He gives a hypothesis regarding a *spiral curriculum:* "[A]ny subject can be taught effectively in some intellectually honest form to any child at any stage of development" (33). He respects a child's ability to understand the same concepts that an adult with years of study knows. The child can be taught scale structure at the beginning of music study by appealing to his way of understanding. He can learn the concept of scale structures by playing five-finger major and minor scales. The student who has studied music for several years gains a more in-depth understanding about scale structures than the child by playing two-octave major, natural minor, harmonic minor, and melodic minor scales. Some students are capable of learning a new concept before it is introduced in the method book, or they may study a previously learned concept more thoroughly. Rather than following the order of presentation in the book for these students, the teacher can adjust the presentation to extend the students' understanding of musical structure when they are ready.

A comprehensive curriculum stresses competence in music fundamentals, technique, and artistry. A comprehensive curriculum prepares a student to hear, sing, write, and perform in the musical language. It encourages creativity to interpret compositions with stylistic awareness and to improvise and compose original compositions as well as those based on a composer's style. It develops proficiency in reading music with ease and harmonizing melodies in traditional and contemporary settings.

In order to develop a comprehensive plan for learning music and performance skills, a curriculum must focus on musical concepts, the elements that are similar in all music and skills played. Eleven music, technique, and artistic concepts and their interrelationships form the basis for the curriculum. The structure of music learned through the relation of concepts is the same for both beginning and advanced levels of study; only the complexity of the concept changes. What becomes important is not only the fact of what is learned, such as that a half note gets two beats, but the conceptual understanding of each element—rhythm has longer and shorter sounds. When teaching a concept, ask yourself, "Am I teaching the concept in a way that will transfer to each piece played?"

The instruction should not only relate to the piece being learned at any given moment, but be presented in a way that the student can apply the concept to all music practiced. A student teacher named Adam introduced crescendo and decrescendo not only as symbols for dynamic changes but also as the rise and fall of the melodic line according to the contour of the pitches. This conceptual understanding helped Megan, his student, shape phrases with crescendo and decrescendo in all music, even when the symbols are not given.

When several different pieces are played at a lesson, transferring a musical concept learned in one piece to other pieces unifies the lesson and reinforces the student's understanding of the concept. After teaching a student to play with a relaxed wrist in an exercise in the technique book, the teacher might remind the student to play with a relaxed wrist in each assignment played at the lesson.

Another way of thinking about conceptual transfer is to teach the concept so that it applies to other skills such as transposing or improvising. Teaching students to read by intervals, rather than by note names, transfers readily to transposing. Guy Duckworth says about transfer,

> Any one concept is necessarily transferred from one skill to the others before it is understood in most of its ramifications; mutually benefiting the understanding and usefulness of each skill, e.g., learning to transpose, improvise, harmonize, and play by ear improves the reading process . . . each skill serves as a vehicle for transferring concepts from one situation to another; thereby affording students with opportunities for conceptualizing musical/technical instruction at the keyboard. (*Keyboard Musician*, 138)

Functional skills, therefore, are most important to include in the curriculum to provide students with learning opportunities for conceptualizing.

By focusing on the eleven musical, technique, and artistic concepts (Chapter 4), the student develops an understanding of the theory beyond the notes. Developing the ability to analyze how concepts of pitch, rhythm, tempo, dynamics, and so on are put together in a composition enables the student to observe similar conceptual relationships in other music.

A music curriculum and a piano method are not the same. Although a method can assist one in teaching the curriculum, it is the material for teaching, not necessarily the way that one teaches a student. With a curriculum, the teacher actively takes charge of the content of the lesson rather than passively "turning the pages" of a method book and correcting mistakes.

The choice of a method book for elementary level students becomes an important decision only after the curriculum for a student is decided. Authors of piano method publications present concepts in a manner that reflects their approach to piano instruction. Too often the teacher becomes dependent on the chosen method to organize the lesson, rather than developing a curriculum that reflects her objectives. Avoid the temptation of letting the method book determine the progression of the lesson. Base each lesson on guiding the student to understand musical concepts.

Reading Approach. As an example of a sound approach to the first years of piano study, I offer the following opinions about reading, technique, and musicality. A comprehensive reading approach stresses hearing pitch direction of up, down, or repeat and high and low pitch range. Training the ear before giving the symbols on the grand staff is paramount for guiding students to hearing what they play. Listening can help guide the student to a natural, injury-free technique. Singing and listening exercises are, therefore, very important. Playing well-known melodies by ear is most enjoyable to the beginning student as well as an excellent aid to aural understanding. The student learns to discriminate between steps and skips and pitch direction of up and down. When the grand staff is introduced, continue to stress the step/skip and directional movement of the melody. At this stage, note names become important only for finding where to begin on the keyboard and for changes outside the five-finger pattern. Too often, naming notes becomes an end in itself rather than an outcome of understanding the intervallic and directional movement of the melody. Check the student's conceptual understanding through transposing the melody. Note names are not helpful to the task, but naming intervals from one note to the next allows one to play the melody in a different key.

The rhythmic approach to reading music is one that develops a sense of pulse. Body movement is the best way to develop pulse awareness and rhythmic understanding. Again, before the symbol is introduced, the student should move to the length of a quarter, half, eighth, dotted quarter, and other rhythms. A counting method of chanting rhythm names, counts, or syllables should be used.

Stephen, an undergraduate pedagogy student, was frustrated that his seven-year-old student, Krystal, was not reading music after a year of lessons. He videotaped Krystal's lessons and, after viewing it, I suggested he either change method books or how he was teaching the material. Krystal is a very active child, so I recommended a method in which she could learn melodies by ear away from the piano through singing and shaping the up-down movement of the melody with her hands or body. Krystal sang well and played the melodies successfully. After a few weeks, she was able to relate the ear training to the grand staff and play with music. When Krystal realized that the notation gave her information to play a melody, she began reading with less effort. She was motivated to learn the symbols once she understood the sound behind the sign.

Cynthia, also an undergraduate pedagogy student, was critical of Tiffany's lack of practice and the mistakes she made at the lesson. They were not enjoying the lessons. After observing her lessons, I asked Cynthia to use the lesson as a guided practice time for Tiffany. She asked questions and was supportive as Tiffany worked through learning a new piece. Cynthia usually counted for her student, but Tiffany continued to make rhythmic mistakes. Although she was reluctant to use body movement, I urged her to have Tiffany clap and move to the beat. After a couple of weeks, the lessons became more enjoyable for both teacher and student and Tiffany made progress. These examples illustrate how using ear training and movement in teaching reading is essential to a successful music curriculum.

Maintain the reading and counting approaches with the more difficult intermediate level literature. Aural training in intervals will enable the intermediate level student to play a melodic line more musically. Pulse consistency will enable the advancing student to analyze more difficult rhythm patterns.

Technique Approach. A healthy technical approach during the first years of piano study should develop habits of injury-free playing. I favor beginning on the black keys with large arm movements and gradually defining the smaller finger movements. Try not to stress legato too soon before the wrists and arms develop ease of movement. Posture and bench height are of utmost importance in developing a well-coordinated technique. To avoid tension in the shoulders, arms, and hands, the bench height should allow the forearm to be level with the keyboard, with the upper arm relaxed from the shoulder. A good method of study serves as a guide to the sophisticated movements required for slur, staccato, legato, repeated notes, and various dynamic levels.

Choosing a Method. Consider the following points in choosing a method. What is the reading and technique approach? How are music theory and history presented? Does the method include ear training, improvisation, transposition, harmonization, and composition? Is the music enjoyable to play? Will the layout and illustrations appeal to the student? Does it include CD or General MIDI accompaniments? Of course, a method may not include all of these items and cannot be all things to all people. Please remember that successful music reading is more dependent on the pedagogy of the teacher than the method chosen. If one has a curriculum of study and a sound pedagogical approach, almost any material can be used.

Curriculum Content. A curriculum can assist the teacher in guiding a student to develop musical artistry and the ability to hear, verbalize, and apply musical concepts of dynamics, articulation, and tempo. It can encourage a student to become knowledgeable about historical information about the composer, period, form, and style. A curriculum requires aural training in rhythmic complexity, melodic and harmonic intervals, harmonic progressions, and tonality of major, minor, modal, and contemporary structures.

A curriculum defines a progressive study of scales, chords, and arpeggios that contribute to the technical and theoretical development of the students. Each level should define a flexible yet comprehensive study of major and minor scales and arpeggios to develop velocity, plus chords with inversions and chord progressions to develop harmonic awareness.

The curriculum outlines assessments of musical concepts through reading, memorizing, transposing, harmonizing, playing by ear, improvising, and composing. These functional skills enable the student to play in a variety of settings: performing in recitals and auditions, accompanying soloists and choirs, playing as part of an ensemble in chamber groups, church groups, and jazz bands. The skills are not only practical but equip the student with musical knowledge and skills to enjoy a lifetime of music participation.

Building a Curriculum. Building a curriculum involves both long-term and short-term goals for teaching. Decide what objectives are important to achieve and how they will be assessed. Decide what fundamental concepts and skills are important to stress at the beginning and intermediate levels. In beginning study, concepts and skills are introduced in a very basic form. The complexity of the very same concepts and skills will be illuminated to the intermediate student.

Next, structure a plan for five or so years and build a sequence of concepts and skills for each year. Table 6.1 is an example of a five-level curriculum that may span four to six years. I emphasize that it is only an example and encourage teachers to develop their own. Each teacher has objectives for students, and each student has reasons for studying piano. Therefore, the curriculum serves as a guideline, but it must be adjusted for each student's needs. If the curriculum is a conceptual one, however, it will adapt to a variety of students whether they are beginning the first or second year of piano study, transferring from another teacher, or advancing into the intermediate and advanced repertoire.

College Class Piano Curriculum. A piano curriculum for the college music major requires specific skills because the graduate will use the piano in the profession.

- Voice majors need the ability to play vocal parts, transpose to accommodate individual voices, accompany rehearsals and performances, and record or sequence accompaniments for rehearsals.
- Instrumental majors need to play a score in preparation for conducting a band or orchestra and play accompaniments for students in a teaching studio.
- Music education majors need piano skills of sight reading to accompany and rehearse vocal parts for classroom singing, harmonization to accompany singing and to compensate for instrumental parts not played, transposition to accommodate voice ranges, improvisation for teaching and accompanying a variety of styles, and technology skills to sequence accompaniments for performance.
- Composition students need piano facility to assist them in composing and in playing their compositions into a music notation program.
- Piano majors need the ability to sight read complex scores, play scales and arpeggios with ease, harmonize lead lines, play by ear, improvise, and transpose.

Piano training assists the music student in understanding music theory because piano class provides hands-on experience with theoretical concepts. Ap-

Table 6.1. Piano Curriculum

	Objectives	Concepts	Skills	Assessment
Level 1	Play with inner hearing of melody and rhythm; play melodies by ear, read Christmas carols; perform short pieces	Pitch up/down, intervals to sixth, note names low C to high C; basic rhythms plus dotted quarter and eighth; play contrasting soft and loud and legato and staccato; major/minor five-finger scales and chords	Read, sing, play by ear, transpose, and improvise in limited range	Performance of two contrasting pieces; clapping rhythms and reading at sight; discriminate between contrasting concepts while listening; theory test on basic concepts
Level 2	Play easier classics. Enjoy jazz, popular, and sacred styles. Major and minor scales and primary chord harmony	Extended pitch range and more complex rhythms. Major/natural minor scales and primary chords	Read, sing, memorize, transpose, and improvise in two-voice and simple harmonic textures	Perform contrasting pieces; clap rhythms and sight read two-part textures; listening test of major, minor, intervals, meter; theory test on major/minor chords, scales
Level 3	Play with interpretive knowledge of balance, contrast, touch, and mood; early intermediate level repertoire; play duet literature	Unlimited pitch and rhythm complexity; major and harmonic minor scales, cross hand arpeggios and primary chord progressions	Read, sing, memorize, transpose, and improvise in two-voice and simple harmonic textures	Perform pieces from several style periods; perform in duet; sight read chordal textures; listening test of previous levels plus rhythmic dictation

Continued on the next page

plying theory concepts to the piano is an excellent assessment of the student's progress in understanding theoretical concepts of key, intervals, harmony, form, style, and rhythm.

To assist the college student in developing competence in playing the piano in such a comprehensive manner, the curriculum should focus on conceptual understanding and be demonstrated with musicality through piano skills of sight reading, transposing, improvising, harmonizing, memorizing, and playing

Table 6.1. *Continued*

| Level 4 | Play intermediate repertoire in all styles with focus on polyphonic music, sonatina literature, lyrical music, and contemporary music; accompany soloists and play in ensemble | Two-octave scales adding melodic minor and arpeggios; secondary and seventh chords; knowledge of interpretive and technical principles; develop problem-solving strategies for practice | Read, memorize, harmonize, improvise in polyphonic, homophonic, and contemporary styles | Perform music from all style periods. Harmonize melodies; improvise in style periods; accompany a soloist and play in ensemble; listening test—identify form, style period, composer; theory test of seventh chords, key signatures |
| Level 5 | Read with appropriate dynamics, voicing, pedal; play middle to late intermediate repertoire; accompany soloists; play creative interpretations in a confident manner | Play scales and chords in all keys with fluency and velocity; modal and other contemporary structures; analyze harmony and form in performance pieces; build dynamic plans by phrase, section, and overall form | Read fluently; memorize with analytical knowledge; improvise and harmonize melodies in various styles | Performance of repertoire; technical ease in scales, arpeggios; interpretive independence; demonstration of reading, transposing, harmonizing; verbal discussion of style, composer, analysis of repertoire; play in a trio |

by ear. The twenty-first-century musician also needs skill in using music technology. The list of skills is very demanding for today's music student. For this reason developing a curriculum based on concepts and the ability to transfer and understand tonality, intervals, harmony, form, style, and rhythm is vital to the success of the student. The requirements can be overwhelming to the student, but with a conceptually based curriculum, students learn that *music is music is music.* Table 6.2 is an example of a college class piano curriculum and is patterned after the requirements at Wichita State University.

Exams. Excellent curricula are available that lead to non-competitive auditions. Those discussed later are the Kansas Music Teachers Association's Music Progressions; the Piano Guild auditions; the Royal Conservatory of Music Ex-

Table 6.2. College Class Piano Curriculum

	Objectives	Concepts	Skills	Assessment
Level 1	Reading and playing from the Grand Staff, up to three lines above and below. Knowledge of the major key signatures through the construction of major scales. Development of finger facility, keyboard topography, and playing simple melodies by ear. Introduction to Musical Instrument Digital Interface (MIDI).	Five-finger major/minor scales and chords. Major tetrachords. Augmented and diminished chords. Pentachord position, hand expansions and finger crossings. Use of pedals. Primary chords and dominant seventh chords. Legato, slow, soft controls.	Read, transpose, play be ear, harmonize, improvise, operate MIDI instruments	Play five-note and eight-note scales and cadences. Sight read and transpose two-part songs in limited range or melodies with primary chord accompaniments. Harmonize melodies with primary chords. Improvise on rhythmic patterns with ostinato accompaniment. Twelve-bar blues. Perform a solo for classmates.
Level 2	Expanded scale and chord vocabulary, introduction of modes in all keys, modal improvisation. Harmonization of a melody in keyboard style without the chord symbols given. Use of the pedals. Introduction to music sequencing and continued study of MIDI functions.	Major and minor (three forms) scales. Inversions of primary chord progressions. All modes and modal harmony. Construction of all types of seventh chords. Legato phrasing, slow-moderate tempi, soft-medium dynamics, voicing between hands.	Read, transpose, play be ear, harmonize, improvise, memorize, two-track sequencing	Play all major and minor scales one octave and cadences. Demonstrate modal scales in all keys and improvise with modal harmony. Sight read and transpose songs with primary chords. Harmonize melodies with primary/secondary chords. Perform solos by memory.

Continued on the next page

aminations; the Royal American Conservatory Examinations; the Associated Board of the Royal Schools of Music examination program; the Music Teachers National Association's Assessment Tools for the Independent Music Teacher and the Music Achievement Award Program; and the Trinity College London examinations (see Web site addresses at the end of the chapter). These programs can serve as models for developing one's own curriculum, or they may provide a

Table 6.2. *Continued*

Level 3	Exploration of contemporary idioms, notation, and preparation for four-part reading. Harmonization includes secondary dominants. Editing of musical sequences, quantizing, and further work with MIDI technology.	Whole-tone, pentatonic, synthetic, and modal scales. Twelve-tone row. Three to four voice reading. Secondary dominants. Seventh chords. Slur, staccato, moderate tempi, medium volumes, accent pedaling.	Read, transpose, play be ear, harmonize, improvise, memorize, four-track sequencing with different voices	Play two-octave major/minor scales and chord progressions with secondary dominants. Demonstrate contemporary scales. Read, transpose, harmonize, and improvise using seventh chords and secondary dominants. Perform a contemporary solo.
Level 4	Emphasis on perfecting sight reading skills and proficient accompanying. Further development of keyboard harmony. Drum machine techniques of looping, quantizing, and editing. Comprehensive exam of four levels and preparation for the Piano Proficiency Examination.	Fluent reading of four-part and accompaniments. Understanding of stylistic elements of all style periods. Fluency in harmonizing at sight. Contrasting touches, cross phrasing between hands, legato pedaling.	Read, transpose, play be ear, harmonize, improvise, sequence drum tracks and sequence an original arrangement	Accompany a soloist, play chorale for group singing and sight read accompaniments and chorales. Play one-octave major/minor scales hands together and cadences with secondary chords. Harmonize melodies by ear and at sight. Improvise in several style periods.

plan of study that would satisfy a teacher's needs for her students. Many of the states affiliated with Music Teachers National Association (MTNA) have comprehensive syllabi that lead to yearly examinations sponsored by the state or local associations.

Kansas Music Teachers Association has a plan of study called Music Progressions that "provides a music event evaluating the progressive growth of all students—those studying music as a hobby as well as those aspiring to enter the music world professionally." The yearly event is non-competitive and serves as a report card for the student, teacher, and parents. The philosophy of the event is to encourage students to do their best in a non-threatening atmosphere. Ten levels guide the student to increasing understanding and facility in the following areas:

1. Performance
2. Music understanding and vocabulary
3. Functional skills
   a. Rhythm and pulse development
   b. Sight playing
   c. Keyboard facility of scales, chords, and arpeggios
4. Written Theory
5. Listening
6. Options are available at the discretion of the student and teacher to demonstrate (a) another solo or a solo on a different instrument, (b) an ensemble, (c) a composition, (d) an improvisation, (e) a book report on a musical subject, (f) a listening project, (g) a lead line harmonized, (h) an artistic project based on a musical subject, (i) electronic skills with MIDI sequencing, (j) transposition, (k) analysis of a composition, or (l) performance of a short lecture recital.

The curriculum is flexible so that teachers and students can align their own plans of study for the year with the Music Progressions curriculum. Students at all levels perform two compositions with one memorized. Students are asked questions about the terms, analysis, and history of the music played. Students clap rhythms and sight read. The keyboard facility is flexible in the initial levels to allow scale choices between five or eight notes, major and/or minor, hands alone or together, and chord shells (for example, C and G) or triads. Although levels three through six require only four to six major and minor scales, the intent is that students learn all scales and then choose four to six to prepare well for the exam. Levels seven through ten require all scales. The progression between levels of chord playing is quite logical beginning with root positions of primary triads in level three, and then moving to chord progressions with inversions. Applied theory emphasizes intervals on the keyboard, inversions of triads and seventh chords, playing melodies by ear with harmony, and playing modes. The theory exam involves identification of notes, rhythms, scales, chords, and key signatures with the addition of analysis of scores in the upper levels. The listening exam is an assessment of the ability to hear intervals, scales, chords, and meter. Recorded examples require students to identity style periods, position of melody, texture of polyphony or homophony, tonality, form, and rhythmic and melodic dictation. The options allow students and teachers to include skills that are of interest to their studios.

The Piano Guild, a division of the American College of Musicians, founded in 1929 by Dr. Irl Allison, has a syllabus available to its members. Auditions are scheduled throughout the nation with the Guild providing adjudicators. Performance is an emphasis but with flexibility to enter plans and choose repertoire that range from requiring only one piece to those that include fifteen to twenty pieces. Students are judged in the areas of accuracy, continuity, phrasing, pedaling, dynamics, rhythm, tempo, tone, interpretation, style, and technique. A variety of programs are available, some of which are memorized programs of one to twenty pieces, unmemorized programs of one to eight pieces, jazz programs, and Diploma programs. Programs are flexible and include technical goals as well as repertoire. Publications of the repertoire and keyboard theory are available for all levels.

The Royal Conservatory of Music opened in Toronto, Ontario, Canada, in September 1887. RCM sponsors examinations three times each year in more than three hundred communities, primarily in Canada. The RCM exams are no longer available in the United States. The Certificate Program encompasses twelve grades from beginning to advanced. In the Practical Examination students are tested on performance of repertoire, studies, and technique as well as satisfying ear training and sight reading requirements. Theory examinations test rudiments, harmony, history, form and analysis, and counterpoint. The various syllabi of the Royal Conservatory of Music Examinations list the requirements for each grade and subject and are published by the Frederick Harris Publishing Company. The syllabi include standard repertoire from the Baroque, Classical, Romantic, and Contemporary style periods and allow choice of examination programs according to individual musical interests and strengths.

The Royal American Conservatory Examinations (RACE), Scott McBride Smith, president, provides a national curriculum and assessment program to American teachers and families, working in cooperation with the Royal Conservatory. The program is similar to the Royal Conservatory program described earlier, with some differences that accommodate the needs of American students and teachers. Additions include two early levels in order for the student in the first year of study to participate, a choice of one piece from any style period, and expansion of the syllabus to include pieces by American composers. The American version continues the rigorous training of examiners to provide a uniform standard and attempts to establish a national standard of excellence in teaching.

The Associated Board of the Royal Schools of Music provides an examination program for all who play musical instruments and provides goals, assessment, and certification of progress at each stage of their development. The Associated Board, which was established in 1889, has the authority of the four leading conservatories in the United Kingdom: the Royal Academy of Music, the Royal College of Music, the Royal Northern College of Music, and the Royal Scottish Academy of Music and Drama. Examination centers are established all over the world with the Associated Board hiring and training the adjudicators. The program is divided into a prep test and grades 1–8. Each grade contains a theory exam. The Practical Musicianship exam includes singing melodies, transposing, and improvising. The Piano Practical exams include prescribed lists of repertoire, an aural exam, sight reading, scales, chords, and arpeggios. A complete copy of the syllabus is posted online.

Music Teachers National Association provides Assessment Tools for the Independent Music Teacher which may be ordered on their Web site. The three tools provide resources for music teachers to do their jobs better and more efficiently: self-assessment, peer assessment, and client assessment. A section of the questionnaires is devoted to curriculum content and serves as an excellent model for developing a comprehensive curriculum.

MTNA also has a Music Achievement Award Program to encourage all students in a teacher's studio to continue their music study and to strive to achieve goals that will not only help them become better musicians, but that will also enhance their love and appreciation of music. Although it is not a curriculum, a teacher could use the award program to give the student recognition for achieving his or her curriculum goals instead of an audition examination. The incentive plan awards MTNA pins after the student achieves the goals set by the teacher over a specified period of time. An implementation packet includes a description of the program and suggestions for goals.

Trinity College London provides examinations at sites in England as well as India, South Africa, Ceylon, New Zealand, and Australia. The music exams are offered in thirty-two instruments as well as voice across nine grades from beginner to accomplished performer. Options in the piano exam include solo, accompanying, duet, and six hands ensemble. Candidates play three or four pieces and take tests in technical work, sight reading, aural awareness, chord progressions, and transposition. Syllabi for all exams are available online, and Trinity publishes repertoire, studies, and sight reading. The listing of objectives for each grade and expected learning outcomes for each level to achieve is especially helpful. The achievement guidelines are intended to help teachers choose repertoire and prepare students for performance with regard to the examiner's expectation. For example, at the entry level students are expected to have acquired a basic technical foundation and demonstrate some interpretation through dynamics and articulation. "They will perform audibly, with a sense of enthusiasm and enjoyment and with some awareness of audience." At the advanced level students are expected to play a secure and sustained performance that demonstrates a mature grasp of the material: "Along with confidence, a sense of ownership and self-awareness, this will result in a discriminating and sensitive personal interpretation that conveys complexity and control of shape (e.g. throughout a sonata movement), and awareness of stylistic interpretation" (54).

In conclusion, I would like to share some thoughts from pedagogy students who have worked with a curriculum for their students for one or two semesters. Most of the student-teachers were in their beginning year of teaching and their students were working on the beginning levels of Music Progressions, the curriculum cited above developed by the Kansas Music Teachers Association. They host the spring Music Progressions examinations held on the Wichita State University campus each year. Each student-teacher enrolls at least one of his or her students in the event.

Luke said, "I think Music Progressions is a great way to develop musicianship in the growing pianist." Several students commented on how the curriculum caused them to be more goal-oriented and prompted them to spend much more time preparing for lessons rather than only relying on the method book to organize lessons. Many felt it improved their teaching and that the curriculum gave them a step-by-step approach which helped to systematically guide them in teaching the student. Joann, a graduate student, described her work with Kara: "I wrote long-range lesson plans beginning with our ultimate goal and worked backwards to ensure that all concepts would be covered by the examination day. We had fun and I felt more focused on strengthening and troubleshooting Kara's skills."

Those with transfer students used the curriculum like an interview to assess the students' progress and needs. Ashley's student, Ellen, had difficulty with sight reading and keeping a steady pulse. Ellen committed to practicing more to prepare for the Music Progressions event, and she made considerable improvement even though she could not attend the event. Andrea described her first month of lessons based on concepts in Music Progressions with an intermediate student, Alexis. "She had been playing chords for a long time, but didn't understand them. Now she's beginning to understand how chord progressions work and is able to identify I, IV, V chords in her pieces. Things are much easier for her. She's playing a Clementi Sonatina with lots of scale patterns and broken chords. Her fingers are flying through the scale patterns and her hands can find the chord positions much faster. We have worked on reading by patterns so her reading has improved and she is much more excited about playing and appreciative of learning music."

Micah sums up how her teaching motivated both students and parents: "Just the words 'Music Progressions' made Mariah feel that something really serious is happening. She began practicing more with the encouragement of Mom and Grandma. It changed both Mariah and her family's perspective and attitude toward the piano and piano lessons."

The act of organizing a curriculum for students is part of the process of guiding the student to musical understanding. Just doing it gives focus to what is important in teaching. It serves as a reminder throughout the year of what concepts or skills have been covered as well as those neglected. Using a curriculum is like using a road map that leads to musical enjoyment and artistry. There are many routes that lead to the same destination, and the journey is what makes teaching so rewarding. Teachers hold precious those moments when we connect with our students and learn something as a teacher from the student's unique way of thinking. A purposeful direction can infuse energy into previously low-key lessons. This kind of enthusiastic lesson is motivating to both student and teacher.

Suggested Resources

Books

Dewey, *School and Society* (1900) and *The Child and the Curriculum* (1902).
Duckworth, "Curriculum from 1968," in *Keyboard Musician*.

Methods Reviewed

Baker-Jordan, *Practical Piano Pedagogy.*
Uszler, Gordon, and Smith, *The Well-Tempered Keyboard Teacher.*

Intermediate and Advanced Literature

Albergo and Alexander, *Intermediate Piano Repertoire.*
Hinson, *Guide to the Pianist's Repertoire.*
Magrath, *The Pianist's Guide to Standard Teaching and Performance Literature.*

Web sites

American College of Musicians, <http://www.pianoguild.com/>
Associated Board of the Royal Schools of Music, <http://www.abrsm.ac.uk./>
Music Teachers National Association, <http://www.mtna.org/>
RCM Examinations, <http://www.rcmexaminations.org/>
Royal American Conservatory Examinations, <http://www.royalamericanconservatory.org/>
Trinity the International Examination Board, <http://www.trinitycollege.co.uk/>

Further Thought

• What essential skills should piano students have?
• How are method books and curricula similar or different?
• How do you adapt a method to your curriculum?
• Why would you have your students participate in curriculum examinations?

7 Communication between Student and Teacher

Seek first to understand, then to be understood.

—Stephen Covey

When I first began teaching piano, I told the student what to play, showed her how to play it, and criticized her for mistakes. M'Lou played well-prepared assignments on the upright piano in the old, dark high school storeroom in Crosbyton, Texas, where I taught lessons. M'Lou did what I told her and never questioned my authority. Sandy, by contrast, seemed to intentionally test me. She failed to practice her assignment and did not follow my directions. The mentor-teacher I assisted gave me a list of progressive punishments for lack of practice with "send the student home" as the most severe. I sent Sandy home. I felt like the meanest person on the planet. Thirty years later I remember Sandy and wish I had another chance to motivate her. I fear that her musical life stopped in third grade rather than maturing into adult enjoyment.

What could I have said in Sandy's lessons to motivate her? I love to meet people and curiously ask them many questions. I could have asked Sandy questions and been curious about her practice. All of my piano teachers encouraged my efforts, so why didn't I encourage Sandy? Surely she did something right; she at least attended lessons.

What a revelation to me when Dr. Guy Duckworth shared interaction analysis with me. He told our class that the resources for learning lie within the student. We ask questions, praise efforts, and build on student's ideas to assess their musical thinking and help them solve problems. Based on the understanding of the student, we decide the course of the lesson and direct their playing. The quote at the start of this chapter, from Stephen Covey's book *The Seven Habits of Highly Effective People*, is good advice for all teachers (237).

Guy told me a story about a psychology professor who analyzed his teaching interaction. Guy taught a group of students for a television series produced by the University of Minnesota in 1958–1959. Ned Flanders, a psychology professor at the University of Minnesota who researched communication patterns in school classrooms, assigned one of his college students to analyze interaction in Guy's televised lessons. Flanders remarked after seeing his student's analysis that Guy's excellent teaching confirmed his theories of balancing dominative influence with integrative influence.

Table 7.1. Key Features of Dominative and Integrative Instruction

	Dominative	**Integrative**
Paradigm	Lecture, model, questions for assessment	Discussion
Communication Mode	Transmit	Transform student's understanding
Source of Knowledge	Teacher, Text	Includes student's interpretations and experience
Student Participation	Restricted	Free

According to Flanders, teachers use dominative influence to express ideas, give directions, express approval or disapproval, and clarify student problems. Integrative influence is used to diagnose feelings and attitudes, ask questions, and apply student answers to the solution of the problem. In Flanders's research, higher student achievement correlated with interaction that encouraged verbal participation and initiative by the students. Dominative patterns restricted freedom of action by the students (14). Table 7.1 highlights the key features of dominative and integrative instruction. Thus, good attitudes and high achievement of Guy's piano students correlated with his balance of integrative and dominative patterns of influence.

Guy taught his pedagogy students to begin the piano lesson with integrative influences (accepting feelings, praising, questioning, and building on the ideas of students). After gathering information from the comments of students, he taught that our teaching influence then moves to dominative influences—directing the lesson, giving opinions, and giving constructive criticism.

Studies on communication show that the majority of talk in the classroom is by the teacher (Booth and Thornley-Hall; Barnes and Todd; Nystrand). Those rare instances when teachers use a discussion approach in the classroom result in higher student achievement and better attitudes about learning. Students tend to be passive and wait for the teacher to pour in knowledge in dominative classrooms. Students are curious, ask more questions, and actively participate in higher-level thinking in integrative classrooms.

Changing one's teaching pattern is difficult and even painful. As a pedagogy student at Colorado, I forced myself to change from directing, lecturing, and criticizing students to asking questions, praising, and building on their ideas. At first I felt very unnatural using integrative influence. Teaching in a conversational manner took away my authoritarian crutch, thus removing my ill-perceived sense of control in the lesson. Teaching piano to college students when I was college-age myself was rather intimidating. Perhaps I felt unnatural asking questions because I was afraid of the answers I would get. As I gained confidence, the integrative pattern became more natural.

My students were more responsive and worked harder in lessons when I asked what practice problems they had and pursued answers to their problems. When I slipped back into a rather non-productive dominative pattern, the students were passive and their performance did not improve. I was not relating to the students.

A suggestion from one of my teachers to help me understand student behavior was that I try to empathize with feelings students were having in learning piano by remembering a time when I had learned something new. Empathizing with feelings of students enabled me to get to know my students and care about them. Relating on an emotional level rather than an intellectual one was an enlightening moment for me.

Teachers may not be aware of communication patterns and how they influence student behavior. Concern about a student's progress is a warning sign to review the teaching manner. More than likely, the interaction pattern could improve. Warning signs are lack of practice, poor reading, repeated mistakes, forgotten dynamics after constant reminders, and dependent or hostile behavior.

To evaluate communication patterns, record a lesson and listen objectively or ask a colleague to observe a lesson and give feedback. Awareness of what is said to students and their response is the first step to improving communication. Experienced as well as inexperienced teachers may feel like reluctant actors on stage while recording a lesson, regarding it as an intrusion on their spontaneity. Inexperienced teachers may feel like the recording is an exam, regarding it as an inhibitor to their teaching and their student's comfort. With repeated recordings and observations, however, the anxiousness wears off and the recorder is ignored. As a teacher in Boulder, I tape-recorded the classes and evaluated my interactions with students. I listened to many lessons while driving from my apartment in Denver to the university in Boulder. Listening to recordings of myself was very uncomfortable, but it was well worth the effort. Self-study of talk patterns and how they affect the student's thinking and playing will assist one's growth as a teacher.

During the past thirty years, I have evaluated my teaching, others' teaching, and asked teachers and pedagogy students to analyze their interaction with their students. Communication is a primary area of concern in the teaching evaluations and the most difficult for teachers to change.

If teachers wish to explore improving communication patterns in order to become more effective in their teaching, this chapter serves as a guide to understanding how what we say affects the student's development.

Table 7.2. Communication Modes in the Lesson

	Direct	Indirect
Teacher Influence	Lecturing	Accepting feelings
	Giving directions	Praising, encouraging
	Criticizing	Building on student's ideas
		Asking questions
Student Participation	Restricted	Freedom to develop opinions

What do teachers say in the lesson? Teachers lecture, criticize, and give directions that are *direct modes* of communicating information and evaluating students. Teachers also ask questions and elaborate on ideas of students. They praise the student's work and acknowledge the student's feelings in the learning process. These are *indirect modes* of communicating with the student. Each mode of interaction influences the student's response. Therefore, I will refer to the direct and indirect modes of communication as *direct and indirect influences* (Table 7.2). Teachers use indirect influence to learn what students think and how they feel about their practice and then turn to direct influence to guide students to elaborate their thinking and improve their performance. Balancing direct and indirect influence encourages participation in the lesson and helps the student to think and solve musical problems.

Although various methods have been devised to classify communication in the classroom, I adapted Ned Flanders's ingenious method of reviewing one's communication using number categories of interaction (34) (Table 7.3). The first seven categories are the indirect and direct influences of the teacher. The remaining three categories are student solicited and unsolicited verbal and musical responses to the teacher, along with a category for silence. I will use these teacher and student talk categories as a springboard for discussing my experience with communication in teaching. In Table 7.3, the categories of influence and a short description of each are given.

I urge you to take a minute to memorize the ten categories and the number associated with each category. It will make the rest of the chapter easier to follow. Also, you will become more aware of the communication patterns in your lessons.

In order to evaluate lessons using interaction analysis, videotape or tape-record the lesson and list numbers that correspond with the type of influence and the student response. I usually list the numbers from left to right, but a ver-

Table 7.3. Categories of Teacher Influence for Interaction Analysis

Indirect Teacher Talk	1	**Accepting feelings**	Teacher nods in understanding, empathizes, and acknowledges emotions and experiences that the student brings to the lesson, whether related to music or not. Says, "I understand. It's hard to practice with such a busy schedule."
	2	**Praising,** **encouraging**	Teacher responds positively when a student plays. Students may not have the musical experience to evaluate themselves and need the feedback of what was well played. Describe to the student what you heard. Start with what was played well or at least what intentions were evident. Encouragement is more of a motivation than criticism. The student must develop an attitude of "I can do it." Describe your praise. "Nice" and "good" aren't descriptive. "Good rhythm" and "You got the notes" address specific concepts. Use humor to relieve tension, but not jokes at the individual's expense.
	3	**Building on** **student's ideas**	Use the student's answer to clarify, develop, and build on concepts being discussed. Use the student's answer to a question or their playing to experiment with the music, then evaluate the result together. Students will make decisions more readily and develop confidence, if they feel the teacher values what they have to say.
	4	**Asking questions**	Asking good questions is an art. Ask open-ended questions with many "correct" answers. Ask questions to direct thinking and assess understanding and knowledge.

Continued on the next page

Table 7.3. *Continued*

			Refrain from asking questions that are actually lectures in which agreement with the teacher is expected. (Don't you think? Don't you agree? Wouldn't you say?) Politely framed directions are not questions. Say, "Turn to page 5" rather than, "Will you turn to page 5?" If the student asks a question, *reverse* the question back to them to answer, *relay* the question to another student, or *answer* the question yourself.
Direct	5	**Lecturing**	Teacher gives information, ideas, and opinions. Lectures should be short and followed by doing what is talked about. Students need your expertise.
Teacher	6	**Giving directions**	Teacher gives directions, commands, or orders with which students are expected to comply. Sample directions are: "Play hands together," "Name the key of the piece," "Bring out the melody," and "Voice to the top note of the chord." Questions that really are directions are ineffective. The question, "Do you have any comments?" usually will get a response of "No." If you really want students to comment, give a specific direction: "Comment on the dynamics that you played."
Talk			
	7	**Criticizing, justifying authority**	Used to correct inappropriate behavior. Used to demand excellence from the student. Always delivered in a constructive, positive, yet commanding tone–never given out of anger or impatience. This approach often entails explaining why the teacher is doing what she is doing.

Table 7.3. *Continued*

Student	8	**Student response–solicited**	The teacher asks a question or gives a direction and the student responds verbally or musically. Freedom of expression is limited.
Talk	9	**Student response–unsolicited**	The student asks questions, gives ideas, or plays without the teacher soliciting the response. Freedom to develop personal opinions and interpretations.
	10	**Silence**	Pauses, short periods of silence, or periods of confusion with neither the teacher nor student talking or playing.

tical listing may be your preference. Record a number every two to three seconds (about twenty-five per minute), and observe the pattern of communication. Note the beginning of each activity and write down significant influences and responses to reflect on later. The student's responses tend to reflect the balance of indirect and direct communication. For instance, if the teacher communicates mainly by direct influence, then the student's verbal or musical response will be compliant. If the teacher's direct and indirect influences are balanced, the student will be actively engaged in the lesson by frequently asking questions and giving comments. The goal is a fifty-fifty balance of indirect and direct comments.

Even more important than analyzing one's teaching is the self-awareness that can come from listening to your own words and observing how the learner responds. Teachers share their knowledge and love of music through playing and telling students about the music. However, instruction by playing and telling does not always work. Each student is unique and perceives and makes decisions in his or her own way. A classic example that you may have seen is the drawing of a woman that illustrates how each person perceives differently (Ex. 7.1). Some see an old woman in the picture and others see a young woman. It takes some effort to explain each other's perception of the woman in order to see each other's point of view. Likewise, in teaching, if the student doesn't understand, consider alternatives such as asking the student to explain or encouraging his questions to help him understand your view.

My primary concern in teaching is to get students to think and to make good musical decisions. I am vigilant to make sure that what I say and do works toward those ends. When I fail, I ask myself why. Was I not aware of the student's

Communication between Student and Teacher 77

Example 7.1. Do you see an old woman or young woman?

feelings? Was I not listening to him? Had I become so absorbed with my agenda that I wasn't aware he wasn't getting it? Analyzing my teaching helps me review the lesson and gives me specific tools to improve.

Following is a discussion of each topic in Table 7.3 with examples from lessons that I have taught or my pedagogy students have taught to explain the categories of influence.

1. **Accepting feelings.** Accepting a student's feelings is an acknowledgment

that you care about them as a person, not just as a performer. A simple "Uh huh" or "Yes, I understand" is all it takes to let the student know you are listening. Accepting feelings requires empathy. Webster's dictionary defines empathy as "the projection of one's own personality into the personality of another in order to understand them better." Think of a time when you had a similar feeling to what the student is experiencing. The situation won't be the same, but you can identify with the feeling.

Petra told me about her experience playing a hymn for church for the first time. On one verse she missed some notes, but she kept the beat and meter going. One of her sixth-grade classmates said, "That was terrible," which hurt Petra's feelings. When she told me about it at her lesson, I responded that I knew how she felt. I shared with her that I began playing for church in junior high school, and I had some similar incidents in learning to play for the congregation's singing. I assured her it gets easier and praised her poise for not stopping when she made a mistake. Six months later, after Petra had played for Mass twice a month, her parents proudly told me about her playing "Silent Night" beautifully for Christmas Eve Mass.

When students fail to practice, they may seem distracted, anxious, and not engaged in the lesson. They feel guilty about not meeting their responsibility. Some will tell me immediately, and others let me discover it. I acknowledge their honesty and share that I understand their feelings. Occasionally, it is not possible for the student to practice consistently. I suggest that the student play music that has not been heard in two weeks or that we work on musicianship skills of ear training, harmonizing, transposing, improvising, and sight reading. There is always plenty to learn! Students are usually relieved that I understand, and they can enjoy the challenge of developing other skills.

If a teacher does not acknowledge the student's feelings, emotions can disrupt the lesson, because the student's energy is directed toward coping with them. Teachers get impatient at times like this and sometimes ignore the student's feelings. Tension develops between teacher and student and little is accomplished in the lesson.

Exchanging greetings when the student arrives can determine how the lesson will go. In her first year of teaching, an instructor named Joan failed to listen to her student, Niall, an eight-year-old beginner. He came bounding into his class of four students declaring that he had memorized "Ode to Joy." Joan was busy beginning the class and did not hear him. About ten minutes later, he announced his accomplishment again and Joan said "Oh" and continued. At this point Niall was fidgeting on the bench, which annoyed the teacher. By the end of the class Niall demanded to play "Ode to Joy" and he did. The hour wait was frustrating to him and made it difficult for him to concentrate on the lesson. Joan admitted she only heard Niall express his excitement of having learned "Ode to Joy" at the end of class.

Engage the students in conversation by looking directly at them. Kneel or sit with younger students to be at eye level with them. Listen intently to what they have to say and appreciate what they offer to you.

2. **Praising, encouraging.** It is human nature to want to feel successful and be praised for doing well. The piano student, after many hours of practice, is delighted with audience applause and positive comments about his performance. Following are suggestions to keep in mind when praising students. Comments are characterized as:

- Specific and immediate
- Descriptive rather than judgmental
- Honest
- Relative to the student's progress on a particular piece
- Encouraging

Positive feedback, given immediately after playing, serves to let the student know that what they intended was heard. Giving specifics of what was good about the playing clarifies concepts that may have been implemented intuitively. Praising the student sets a positive tone for the lesson. Praise may be for good intentions even when the technique or other problems are interfering with a solid, convincing performance. A student who intuitively plays rubato in a romantic character piece may be praised for her sensitivity even though she may not be able to give a musical reason for her exaggerated rubato. Positive reinforcement about a fine performance or even one that is flawed encourages the student to work to make the lesson productive.

Effective praise is descriptive rather than judgmental. Describing the student's sound gives more information about how the music was played rather than judging the accuracy of the playing. A descriptive comment such as "The staccatos were very short and light throughout" tells the student that the interpretation was heard. A judgmental comment such as "I loved the staccatos" is less productive because the personal reaction lacks a description of the sound of the staccatos.

The adjective "good" is so overused that it ceases to have meaning, and it often means something completely different than a word describing the performance. "Good" sometimes means the end of a topic as in the following teacher's comment. "Practice increasing the tempo for next week. Good. Now play the Sonatina." "Good" is often used to acknowledge good and bad playing. Even if the playing is poor, "good" begins the sentence before the real critique begins. Or worse yet, the teacher says "good" and goes on to the next item on the lesson notebook without improving the playing. We send a message to the student that sloppy playing is "good," when he knows that he did not practice or play his best. Rather than praise poor playing, acknowledge feelings of the student: "I know you are concerned that your playing was not your best."

Dishonest praise can undermine the trust a student has in the teacher. If a student continually hears that anything she does is okay when it is not, she will lose confidence in the teacher and lose motivation to do her best in practice and lessons. Some students will disregard nearly any praise because they are never satisfied with their playing and have trouble accepting honest praise. However, in both cases give a detailed description of the playing so students will understand the well-deserved praise.

Positive comments are relative to the stage of preparation of the composition. A positive reaction to an initially correct reading of notes and rhythms assures students that with practice they are capable of giving a fine performance. However, after a month the reading should be more accurate with a more knowledgeable rendition of the style.

Kind words of encouragement rather than criticism may help a student learn who is resistant to instruction. Some college students in required piano classes would rather not be at the lesson. Try to find out the reason for the attitude that prevents the student from learning. His resistant attitude may be from a misunderstanding or perhaps a lack of confidence in playing the piano. He needs encouragement to help him believe he is capable. Ted, a voice major in a college piano class that I taught, asked cynical questions and often had me repeat a statement. His behavior shouted, "I do not want to be in piano class!" Instead of reacting defensively, I responded with kind words and gave him assistance to play what was required. He finally opened up and said he had a 30 percent hearing loss. I was careful thereafter to make sure Ted heard the directions and assignments. He responded with a positive attitude about learning and practiced his assignments effectively.

Teaching is an art and part of the art is praising in a clear, descriptive way. Encouragement serves to clarify what was played well, motivate further thoughtful practice, and build confidence.

3. **Building on student's ideas.** The student will make decisions more readily if she feels the teacher values what she has to say. Building on a student's answer is one of my most used strategies in lessons. It encourages the student to be active rather than passive. It often sparks an enthusiasm for the music that she didn't have in the previous week's practice. I get to see impressions of the wonderful piano literature afresh through the student's eyes. I prod them to teach themselves by figuring out a note they missed or by listening to their pulse in a difficult rhythm passage. I delight when they bring the music to life after asking them to decide upon and explain the emotion or mood that they perceive.

To elicit such behavior, listen to a response to a question or an unsolicited response and build on the idea. Lead her to correct a mistake or to understand a new concept by asking her to explain what she knows. If she has to figure out the correct note, she is more likely to remember it every time she plays. By contrast, if she is told what the note is, she may still play with mistakes.

Some students would rather play what they mean rather than verbalize their understanding. If they aren't used to speaking in lessons, it may take a while for them to adjust to expressing themselves. In a conversational relationship, a teacher is primarily interested in the student's perception of a problem and in helping the student experiment with solutions to the problem. Students are required to use higher-level thinking skills in such a lesson, and that will translate to successful practice sessions.

The lesson environment is one in which students learn to listen, understand, and make informed decisions about the performance of music. Students learn to take chances, try different approaches, follow their intuitions, and use their present knowledge in order to solve problems.

Teachers' reactions to student responses can positively or negatively affect their thinking during practice. If we criticize them for what we think is an incorrect opinion or ignore the response and have them do it our way, then the student will remain reluctant to give opinions. Consider the following scenario.

Act One *1st Draft*
A student has played Prelude in E Minor by Chopin in a fast tempo, but it is marked largo. The teacher paces back and forth and is visibly upset with the performance.

Teacher: (*irritated*) What is the mood of this piece?
Student: (*hesitates and timidly answers*) Lively.
Teacher: (*raising her voice*) No, it is a somber mood because of the slow tempo marking.
Student: (*looks down, hurt*)

Act One *2nd Draft*
A student has played Prelude in E Minor by Chopin in a fast tempo, but it is marked largo. The teacher is surprised that the advancing student has failed to observe the tempo marking. She plans quickly, hoping to guide the student to reconsider her tempo choice.

Teacher: (*interestedly*) What is the tempo of this piece?
Student: (*without hesitation*) Lively.
Teacher: (*curiously*) What clues do you have that it is a lively mood?
Student: The left hand has fast eighth-note chords.
Teacher: Ah, I see what you mean. (*considers the point-of-view of the student*) The repeated chords do look busy. Does the tempo marking support fast chords?
Student: (*thoughtfully*) Hum, largo, rather slow. Maybe it's not so lively.
Teacher: What is the key?
Student: (*silently analyzes the key*) E minor.
Teacher: What mood might better describe a slow piece in a minor key?
Student: It's not really sad because the accompaniment really moves. Maybe gentle and reflective. The dynamic marking is expressive and the legato melody has long notes that repeat, just like someone is reflecting on the past.

The first draft of Act 1 had an unfortunate ending, whereas the second draft ended with the teacher and student engaged in conversation, with positive results from the student's insight into the interpretation of the *Prelude*. The teacher used the response of "lively" to engage the student in conversation. The questions helped her think of a better mood description according to what she saw in the score. Although asking questions took more time than giving instructions, the student learned more because she had to gather evidence from the piece. After being asked questions about the tempo and key, the student began thinking and discovered that besides the tempo and key, the dynamic and touch markings and pitch patterns suggested a different mood than her first impression.

In order to help students learn to make musical decisions, listen to their responses and lead them to improve their performance based on those responses. Students will gain confidence in expressing opinions that will help them solve problems independently.

4. **Asking questions.** Asking a good question is just as important to the teacher as playing a beautiful phrase is to the performer. Questions require students to think and make decisions about the music leading to insightful discoveries about the composer's meaning. Since we are teaching the student, not just the materials, questions help us assess their understanding and give direction to the lesson. Questions help teachers avoid having students who respond with mindless imitation. Open-ended and probing questions require the student to form opinions and make decisions.

Some questions are used to assess understanding and to encourage students to think before playing. "What is the key of the piece? What finger in the left hand begins the B flat major scale? Where does the second theme of the sonata begin?" All of these questions require a factual answer. If the student does not respond with the correct answer, assist the student in his reasoning to find the answer.

Open-ended questions with many possible answers provide fertile ground to help students solve problems independently. They guide students to understand music and require them to think, to sort out the possibilities, and to arrive at possible solutions. The intention is not to prod students to answer "correctly," but to plant thought-provoking ideas about the construction of the music. A question such as "What are the similarities in the music?" may raise awareness of repeated pitch and rhythm patterns. Likewise, a question of "What are the differences?" might prompt recognition of changes of texture, articulation, and harmony. When students are led to understand the structure of music, they begin to see "inside" the music, which assists them in playing with ease and musicality.

Students must be given time to answer questions. Be careful not to answer your own question if students do not respond immediately. I was alarmed by the interaction of a student teacher with her student in a master class. After Angela played, Diane asked her the following questions: "Angela, what about the accents, the dynamics? What about the tempo? Was it too fast?" Diane asked one question after another without giving Angela time to answer. The questions were good ones for making the student think. Rather than wanting an answer, however, the teacher's manner in asking the questions was to criticize Angela for not following accent and dynamic markings and for playing too fast. Instead of critiquing the student, ask questions that guide a student to make her own critique, which leaves a more lasting impression. Don't ask a question if you intend to tell the student what to do. Perhaps she wanted Angela to think about the dynamics. More appropriate is a direction such as "Think about the accents, dynamics, and tempo in the music."

Asking questions before the lesson begins may also be very effective. At the outset of the lesson, ask the student what he accomplished during practice. Students may share practice and lesson problems that can be resolved. Sometimes I spend so much lesson time on festival or contest literature that I neglect the rest of the assignment. Uta, a talented eighth grader, was concentrating on Debussy's "Snow Is Dancing" for a festival, but she had many other compositions she practiced at home. The Debussy had dominated lesson time for over a month, and I had not heard other assignments. I asked if she would like to play the Bach dances, Chopin Nocturne, and the lead line harmonization from her assignment. She looked relieved and said yes. She had been playing the Bach for two to three months and was ready for a new assignment. I listened to her entire assignment, made a new assignment, and still had half the lesson for the Debussy. The lesson plan was determined by asking Uta a question, which led to a fruitful direction. As a result, she began her week of practice with renewed motivation.

Changing one's style of communication takes study and planning. Betty was motivated to change because joy and creativity seemed to be missing in seven-year-old Cori and Colton's lessons. They were very conscientious students and much was accomplished in the well-planned lessons, but they seemed nervous and distracted. Her lessons with Cori and Colton had a serious tone with the students doing what Betty asked. Eventually Betty changed her interaction and tried to relax the students through questions, humor from the funny titles in their books, and eurhythmics. The students' demeanor changed and they seemed to enjoy participating in the activities, thinking, and learning. Her initial goals for teaching the children were mainly about what materials she would cover. Betty became more perceptive about the students' feelings and less concerned with the songs to be perfected for the recital. She was reminded of some words of wisdom that she heard at a session of a Music Teachers National Association Convention: "Trust and care that each person wants to learn. Students don't care until they know you care."

I feel I have reached a milestone in lessons when a student is so curious and thoughtful about the music that they initiate questions. I consider such moments golden opportunities to delve into the inner contents of the music. When a student asks a question, three effective strategies are: (1) answer with a reverse question: "What do you think the answer is?" (2) answer with a relay of the question to another student if lessons are in groups: "Bob, could you answer Ann's question?" or (3) answer the question yourself (Fig. 7.1).

The first strategy is to reverse the question and direct students to answer their own questions. The student's response helps the teacher fill the gaps of what the pupil doesn't understand. Uta asked me how to spell seventh chords which is a requirement in a state association's curriculum for preparatory students. Instead

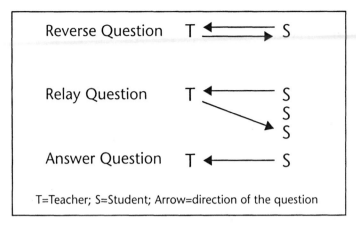

Reverse Question	T ⟷	S
Relay Question	T ⟵	S
		S
		S
Answer Question	T ⟵	S

T=Teacher; S=Student; Arrow=direction of the question

Figure 7.1. Answering Questions to Help Students Think

of spelling the chords for her, I reversed the question and had her spell the chords. She was confused about the triad spelling versus the seventh interval spelling. I provided her a seventh chord chart, and she spelled and played dominant, major, minor, half diminished, and diminished sevenths. Uta already understood intervals and triads. What she learned in the lesson was the proper combination of triads and seventh intervals for the various seventh chords. The question reversal gave Uta the information she needed, rather than my wasting time lecturing on what she already knew.

A variation of a reverse question can help the student answer his own questions. Nine-year-old Paul asked, "What is the first note?" I never answer with the name of the note. Instead, I asked Paul to find the answer and asked more questions to guide his thinking. "Is it treble or bass clef? Is it above or below the landmark G in treble clef? Go up each line and space in the musical alphabet until you find it." Teachers give cues to help students find answers.

The second strategy, to be used in a group setting, is to relay the question to another student in the group. A relay question encourages students to be involved in each other's learning. When they answer a peer's question, their understanding is strengthened. Patricia, a beginning college student, asked Eric, her piano class teacher, "Should the foot go down on the pedal when the chord is played?" Eric directed another student to demonstrate legato pedaling in a pattern of successive chords. Patricia observed when the foot was lowered or raised to get a legato connection and was able to verbalize her understanding.

The third strategy, answering the student's question, is unfortunately the most used option. If students are guided to think about the answers, they can solidify their understanding rather than passively accepting the teacher's answer. However, sometimes answering the question is the best option. Students may not have the knowledge to answer their own questions or those of their peers. For instance, what if a student asked, "Why does Bach's music sound so different from Mozart's?" This is a jewel of a moment to help the student understand musical style. I would pull out scores of Bach and Mozart's music and offer my answer by demonstration and short lecture, and I would encourage the student to contrast the two scores and ask him to offer his insights.

Teachers who ask good questions demonstrate that they care more about the student and his learning than the materials to be learned. The effort teachers spend in planning and asking good questions is well worth it when students exhibit consistent progress and offer musical insights.

5. **Lecturing.** Lecturing is best used at the beginning of a lesson to let students know the plan for the day and at the end of a lesson to summarize what was learned. To begin a group lesson give an overview of what will be learned. In the individual lesson, give an evaluation of the performance and intended direction of the lesson. In both settings proceed with a concrete experience on the topic by asking questions and giving directions. Then end the lesson by summarizing the primary points so the student will remember what to practice.

Telling the student to go home and practice what you have lectured about is rarely productive. The same mistakes may be practiced. Ensure that the student will practice correctly by trying it at the lesson. Model the suggestion at the piano and have the student imitate. Break the concept into smaller parts and give specific directions for the student to apply to the piano. For instance, direct a student having trouble with balance of an Alberti bass and melody to play hands separately. Play the melody *forte,* then the accompaniment as softly as possible. The Alberti bass may need further work to lighten the thumb in the repeated notes while shaping the bass line. Join him in a duet of the two parts or sing together the part not played. Successful experiences at the lesson will enable the student to practice effectively at home.

Limit the lecture to one or two concepts at a time. In evaluating a student's performance, teachers make the mistake of commenting on everything that needs improvement. "The accompaniment was too loud. The melody should end softly. The fingering was not correct in the second measure. The staccatos weren't observed in the second measure." Correcting everything overwhelms the student. Instead work on one concept at a time, even if the student makes other mistakes. If the beginning student is missing notes, allow inaccurate rhythms and focus on intervals. By taking the time to provide students with a "hands-on" experience with a few concepts, teachers can be assured that the student will practice what was discussed.

A time-efficient approach is to ask the student to evaluate the playing and cite problems he has. If the student is aware of the problems, you can get right to work without spending time pointing out weaknesses.

"My teaching has become more than listening and instructing," according to a college student in her third year of teaching. She says she recognizes a student's understanding of problems, has learned how to ask good questions, and has helped the student improve. Inexperienced teachers are often surprised that they primarily use the telling mode of instruction in their lessons. Telling the student everything we know about the subject is not teaching. Of utmost importance is to seek to understand the student's thinking. The teacher said she wanted to "recognize the students' understanding." What a profound, unselfish approach that she can get into the student's skin and figure out what she is thinking.

Excessive lecturing and criticizing may cause tension between teacher and student. Try balancing these direct comments with questions and praise the student when they try and succeed in their attempts. Encouragement might break the ice and motivate the student to try rather than give up out of frustration.

Try to turn lectures into questions that will make the student think. An experienced teacher asked for guidance in teaching Beethoven's Sonata, Op. 49, No. 1 to a high school junior. After evaluating her approach to correcting rhythm inaccuracies, I suggested she ask questions that require the student to make decisions about the music. For example, "Listen to how you played the first theme. Was your rhythm correct?" If she says yes, and it was incorrect, have her write in the counts, count out loud, or play the incorrect rhythm for her while she counts and evaluates the accuracy. The key to good teaching is to be persistent in making the student think. Use questions instead of lectures to make sure they think.

In summary, you can improve lectures by limiting the number of concepts discussed. Balance lectures and criticisms with praise and questions. Effective teaching requires students to make decisions about the music. Training students to think independently is best achieved by balancing direct modes of teaching with indirect ones.

6. **Giving directions.** Teachers give directions to select what will be played from repertoire, lesson, and theory books. We give directions about how to play. In reading new repertoire we direct students to play slowly, carefully, with correct fingering, and without mistakes in notes and rhythms. We direct students to observe tempo, articulation, and dynamic markings. We direct them to give the key signature, play the scale, and observe key changes. After hearing the performance, we direct students to define the form, play musically, balance the melody and accompaniment, and use the arms, elbows, wrists, and fingers effectively to play with ease.

Directions enable teachers to use time efficiently. Giving a short direction instead of a longer lecture keeps the lesson moving with a maximum of playing and a minimum of teacher talk. Directions can be given while the student plays. Directions require the student to react immediately to change. Students have to think and put to use their perception of the direction.

Be careful not to give a direction as a question. Instead of asking, "Will someone identify the key of this piece?" give a direction: "Identify the key of this piece." A student can easily answer "No" to the first question. Give the student a direction so that he is required to answer.

A student-teacher used directions and questions effectively in teaching eight-year-old students to transpose. She began with a lecture on transposition. "Transpose means to perform at a pitch other than the original." She guided the students through a concrete experience by using directions and questions effectively.

Teacher: Write in the key of the piece.
Students wrote key.
Teacher: Name the five-finger scale that you will transpose to.
Students had to make a decision about what scales they knew and select one.
Teacher: Sing and shape the melodic contour of the piece.
Students sang and shaped the steps, skips, repeats in the air.
Teacher: Play the melody in the new key.
Students played.
Teacher: Describe how to transpose.
Students discussed how they transposed.

The teacher gave the students a concrete experience with the new concept by directing them through the lesson. Students were participating each step of the way. The teacher's scheme of interaction was to tell the students the goal of learning to transpose, to guide them through an experience, and to verify their understanding with their own definition of transposition.

Good directions are necessary to involve students in problem solving. Directions guide students through the learning process. Directions immerse students in a learning experience and encourage them to make their own discoveries about music concepts.

7. **Criticizing, justifying authority.** It is easy to tell students what they did wrong and make the correction. It is difficult to give constructive criticism without offending the student. Criticizing the playing and not the performer is a delicate interaction. The student may feel vulnerable and not be able to do his best. More experienced, confident students can handle criticism and learn from the critique. They know they can play well and that they can decide to use or not use the comments. However, most young students, college-age included, do not yet have the positive performance experiences or the knowledge about playing the piano to always respond well to criticism.

It is human nature to be motivated by encouragement rather than criticism. Encouragement builds students' self-esteem and trust. A positive tone in the lesson transfers to positive practice sessions. If a student is told consistently that he is capable, he will come to believe he is capable. If we appreciate our students' efforts and reward them with kind words, they will give more effort.

A rule of thumb in evaluating a student's work is to describe rather than judge the playing. A judgment would be, "You played the piece too fast!" A description would be, "The piece is marked allegretto, but your tempo was presto." The descriptive statement reminds the student about the allegretto tempo marking and tells her that the tempo played was faster. The descriptive statement places the responsibility on the student to change. The judging comment does not require the student to evaluate her own choice of tempo since the teacher does it for her.

The teacher-student relationship is one of developing trust. The teacher trusts that the student can learn and wants to learn. The student trusts that the teacher will treat him with respect and will help him be successful. When trust develops, both teacher and student can voice opinions. In fact, the most productive lessons occur when we reach this level of communication. The teacher can demand excellence from the student by saying, "No, you did not do it. You can do better. Try again." In a lesson on Sergei Prokofiev's Toccata, Op. 11, which is a thrilling and difficult piece, Carter had trouble playing with a sense of forward motion. The teacher and student's relationship had developed over many years to unconditional trust. The intensity of the lesson was striking. The teacher talked over his playing, demanded he play with more drive, started again if he lacked energy, and encouraged him when he got it. The teacher and student were completely focused on the music and the intensity of the moment.

At all times treat the student with respect. At all times demand a high level of excellence from the student. At all times expect the student to give his best effort. Teachers have a myriad of interactions to do this. The balance of indirect and direct influence is the key to teaching in this manner.

8. **Student responses—solicited.** In a solicited response, the student answers questions, follows directions, and plays. Most responses in a lesson are solicited ones. Freedom of expression is limited because the teacher is usually soliciting a correct answer. If the teacher is using direct influence—direction, lecture, and criticism—the student's response is by playing. However, a direction could be used to solicit verbal answers from the student such as "Describe the rhythm patterns of the mazurka." If the teacher is using indirect influence—questions, praise, and encouragement—then the student's response may either be verbal or by playing.

9. **Student responses—unsolicited.** In an unsolicited response the student asks questions, gives ideas, or plays without the teacher soliciting the response. Encouraging dialogue with the student allows him the freedom to develop personal opinions and interpretations. Less than 10 percent of student responses are unsolicited. The student may ask a question, give an opinion or idea, or share an experience. These unsolicited responses tend to occur more often when the teacher has used indirect influence such as building on the student's idea, praising or encouraging the student, and accepting the student's feelings. Asking open-ended questions tends to lead to a conversation in which students freely express themselves.

Unsolicited responses signify that the student is thinking and actively involved in the lesson. A dialogue between teacher and student will motivate her to practice thoughtfully. Interaction analysis using the numbered categories might be as follows. The student's comment (9) is unsolicited and not in answer to a question or direction. The teacher responds by acknowledging and building on the student's comment (3), and then a conversation ensues with both the teacher (5) and the student (9) giving their opinions. I am delighted when this happens in a lesson and consider such times as my most effective teaching.

Because a goal in teaching music is to help students develop an expressive and unique voice through their performance, it seems to me that teachers need to encourage students to give their opinions during instruction. If indirect influence can promote such expression, perhaps students will carry that absorption in the music with them to their performance.

10. **Silence.** Pauses and short periods of silence often mean the student is thinking through the problem. Some students want to think about their answer before responding. Allow enough time for them to answer, even as long as ten seconds. Silence at other times may indicate confusion and is a signal that a different approach is needed. Simply asking if the students understand will clarify why they are silent.

Patterns of Influence

Following are descriptions of some common communication patterns and their strengths and weaknesses. By recording the number corresponding with the seven teacher influences and the two student responses, one can observe communication patterns. Please review the numbers related to each category of interaction analysis.

Critical Pattern. A dialogue is described below of a critical pattern between the teacher and his student. Ashley, a seventh grader, played the Mozart *Theme and Variations* ("Ah, vous dirai-je, Maman"). In the last variation she stumbled through the ending. She played the other variations fairly well and seemed to enjoy playing them. She was outgoing in discussing the piece. Her manner changed dramatically when the teacher criticized her for not practicing enough to play without stumbling.

(4) Teacher: You got to the end. How long have we had this piece?

(8) Ashley: (*Anticipating criticism.*) Forever.

(7) Teacher: No. Five weeks. It doesn't seem like you have made a lot of progress.

(8) (*Ashley fidgets, looks dejected.*)

(4) Teacher: What do you think?

(8) (*Ashley shrugs her shoulders.*)

(2) Teacher: That part sounds good. (*He then points to the part Ashley stumbled through.*)

(7) How much time have you spent on this part? (*Criticism stated as an accusing question.*)

(8) Ashley: I don't know, five or ten minutes. (*She doodles at the piano.*)

(7) Teacher: (*Accusingly*) Do you really spend five to ten minutes on that part right there every time you practice?

(8) (*Ashley nods defensively.*)

(7) Teacher: Do you have a stopwatch? Time it because I don't think you've been spending quite that much time.

(5) Teacher: When you first started this piece, I wasn't worried about you getting it learned, but now I'm worried. We're going to have to do double time now to get it ready, because we're going to play it in a month.

I disagree with the teacher's approach to motivating her to practice. The communication pattern is unbalanced with six direct comments compared to three indirect comments. I would suggest that the teacher ask Ashley how she would improve the piece. Ashley's response would preserve her integrity and give her the responsibility of deciding how to practice.

Question-Answer Pattern. In the next scenario, the teacher asks too many questions that have only one answer. Ask questions that make the student think rather than factual questions that solicit only one correct answer. Following is an excerpt from a lesson illustrating a question approach that requires that the student guess the correct answer.

(4) Teacher: Why do you think you have to use good fingering—the fingering that the score says rather than any finger you want?
(8) Christin: So it's not sloppy?
(4) Teacher: Maybe, but what else? Do you have any other ideas?
(8) Christin: (*She shrugs her shoulders.*)
(4) Teacher: How are we supposed to be playing? (*She points to the slurs.*)
(8) Christin: Soft?
(4) Teacher: Medium soft. What else? What do those mean? (*She points again to the slur markings.*)
(8) Christin: Um. Like.
(7) Teacher: We just talked about it. (*Indignantly*)
(4) They are called slurs. And they mean to play? (*She wanted the student to fill in the blank.*)
(8) Christin: Gently?
(3) Teacher: Gently. It could mean that, but it means something a little bit different from that.
(9) Christin: Smooth?
(2) Teacher: Yes, that's it!
(5) (*The teacher lectures and demonstrates the smooth fingering.*)

The teacher asks a question with only one answer, the one that she wants. This is a disguised lecture. She really wants to tell Christin that a smooth legato is the reason for good fingering. Telling her rather than asking questions would be more honest and efficient in this instance. Christin always gave her answer as if asking, "Is that the right answer?" She knew all along that she had to guess the teacher's answer. The question approach could work well if the teacher had accepted "sloppy, soft, and gently" as good reasons for playing with good fingering and built on Christin's ideas. Although the questions only took a minute of the lesson, I fear Christin may become dependent on her teacher, rather than thinking for herself.

Balanced Communication Pattern. The teacher in the next scenario achieves the goal of a fifty-fifty balance of direct and indirect comments in order to encourage students to think. The teacher begins the lesson by reviewing a five-finger scale.

(6) Teacher: Say the letter names.

(8) Students: G flat A flat B flat C flat D flat (*Students say letter names while looking at the music and playing the G flat pentachord.*)

(9) Emmanuel: (*Pointing to the B flat*) That's a B flat!

(3) Teacher: That's right. In music flat signs look like a small b.

(9) Emmanuel: It looks like a capital B that got squashed.

(9) Brandon: (*Physically shows with both hands a big B being squashed to a little b.*)

(1) Teacher: That makes sense.

(9) Brandon: It got smaller.

(6) Teacher: Now say the letter names.

The directions to name letters and the supportive comments prompted the six-year-old students to discuss how a flat sign looks. The teacher's speech pattern encouraged the six-year-olds' spontaneous and amusing discussion. Notice how the students were at ease to talk about the music. Their comfort is a result of the teacher's willingness to accept their answers and to step back while they learn.

A graduate student, Angela, evaluated her communication patterns in teaching a piano class for college piano majors after working with them for a semester.

> I feel that my greatest teaching strengths are my outgoing personality and listening skills. I try to listen to my students' questions or statements and respond as clearly as possible. When I don't know the answer, I turn the question back to the class for discussion. We always came up with an answer together during the semester. I think it was comforting to the class that the teacher doesn't always know all the answers. I feel that by the end of the class, the students were thinking for themselves and developing their own learning process. They became less dependent on me. I feel that my teaching with this particular class has been very effective and I've enjoyed this class very much. One weakness that could be improved is awareness of when to be indirect or direct based upon the amount of time available in class. For example, towards the end of the semester I was running out of time because I was allowing too much input from the students (indirect). Knowing when to change to a more direct approach, without being coached, would be an effective tool in group teaching.

Angela's evaluation of her teaching shows that she is becoming a very aware and caring educator.

Conclusion. Improvement of teaching effectiveness is in part becoming aware of what you are doing and how it contributes to the productivity of the lesson. Teachers learn through experience and constant evaluation of their effectiveness. Video review of lessons, frequent talks with parents, and critiques of your students' playing in festivals are ways to evaluate your teaching effectiveness. Beginning teachers can learn by attending pedagogy classes, conferences, and workshops. A mentor relationship with an experienced teacher is invaluable. To learn about child development and psychology, consider course work in these areas or ask experts to talk to your music association. Read articles in journals, not only in music performance and music education but also in education and psychology.

If indirect influence is new to your teaching, expect different behaviors from both yourself and the student. The student may be shy at first and reluctant to answer questions. Wait for him to respond. With persistence in asking questions and expecting answers, the student will come prepared to respond. Students will participate more as a result of your flexible communication pattern and take more responsibility for their learning.

Suggested Reading

The following books stress that students use higher-level thinking when oral communication is encouraged in the classroom. Although several of the authors are English or communication teachers, music teachers can easily adapt the principles to music lessons.

Barnes and Todd, *Communication and Learning Revisited: Making Meaning through Talk.*
Booth and Thornley-Hall, eds. *Classroom Talk.*
Covey, *The Seven Habits of Highly Effective People.*
Duke, *Intelligent Music Teaching.*
——, "Teachers' Verbal Corrections and Observers' Perceptions of Teaching and Learning."
Flanders, *Analyzing Teaching Behavior.*
Nystrand, *Opening Dialogue.*

Further Thought

- Why is the way we communicate important?
- Make up questions that will get more than a factual, one-word answer.
- Give some examples of using a student's comment to begin a conversation on the topic.
- What patterns of interaction encourage independent thinking?
- Do interaction analysis on a video of your teaching. Compare the number of indirect influences to direct influences. Did you have a fifty-fifty balance?

8 Learning Styles

When a new student comes for the first lesson with a teacher, there is a period of getting acquainted. Students often want to talk about activities, friends, teachers, pets, and siblings. Older students and adults also tell teachers about their lives. These get-acquainted meetings are important for establishing rapport in order to work together at the piano. After a few weeks of getting to know one another have passed, teachers and students begin to notice differences in the way tasks are accomplished. The teacher may write a detailed assignment, but the student may admit he did not read it during the week. Or perhaps another teacher may have assigned the student to make up a piece about his pet but the student complained that he did not know what notes to play. Teachers often say, "I told you several times to correct that note." Why is it that the student doesn't play it correctly at the next lesson? Why is it that some students seem to always be prepared and yet others don't respond to directions or corrections that teachers give?

Every student has a distinctly individual learning style, and every teacher has a distinctly individual teaching style. Observing a student's preferred learning modality and preferred learning style could help teachers create different approaches when the student does not comprehend the initial instruction.

Learning Modalities. In this scenario, the student was not responding with the correct note after being told repeatedly what to play. In this instance, the teacher may be talking too much rather than having the student try out the correction at the piano. This student may learn by playing rather than by hearing about the correct way to play. For instance, Greg, a student in a college piano class, does not seem to hear me when I introduce a concept, yet he readily understands if he can play while the concept is being discussed. Greg needs to be physically involved when he learns. Other students need to see what is being discussed rather than be told about it. Shannon, also a student in a college piano class, requires that I write her assignment so that she can see it when she practices. Yet another student in the class, Shawn, often says, "Tell me what to work on!" or "Tell me how to do it." She often sings while she plays and obviously prefers listening to instruction.

Greg, Shannon, and Shawn were expressing their preferred mode of learning in their response to my teaching. The three modes of sensory perception are visual, auditory, and kinesthetic. Students have preferred ways of learning in which they perceive, interact with, and respond to the learning environment most naturally. Some learn best by seeing, some by hearing, and others by doing.

According to Walter Barbe and Raymond Swassing's research, the majority of children in sixth grade show a preference for visual learning, after an initial

Figure 8.1. Learning Modalities

Visual	Learns by seeing, watching demonstrations, reading assignments. Likes flashcards. Responds to a visually pleasing environment. Stress note and rhythm patterns for effective reading and memorizing.
Auditory	Learns by hearing verbal instructions. Likes to be told about the assignment. The teacher can play for them, direct their attention to hearing their own playing, and suggest listening to recordings of themselves and others. Counting out loud and verbalizing what they see helps this student.
Kinesthetic	Learns by doing. May be fidgety on the bench and needs to move around the room. Gestures while talking and taps feet or nods head to the beat. Likes hands-on experiences of immediately trying what is talked about. Whole body movement such as eurythmics helps this student.

auditory preference in earlier grades. Kinesthetic learning preferences grow from least preferred in kindergarten to a close second to visual by the time a child reaches sixth grade. About 30 percent of children have mixed strengths and are equally adept at all modes of learning (*Teaching,* 52). Figure 8.1 lists behaviors that are common to each modality preference.

Teachers introduce new concepts most often by using their own preferred modality. However, modality intervention is needed when a student does not understand the concept from the first presentation. Rather than just correcting mistakes, teachers can change the presentation to adapt to the student's modality preference. The teacher can adjust to help the student understand, while preserving the student's integrity and belief that he can be successful.

Personalizing instruction through modality strengths enhances motivation. Shawn wanted me to respond verbally because she prefers the auditory sensory mode. Unfortunately, I wrote out her assignment rather than telling her what it was, and she was not prepared at the next lesson. When I realized her auditory preference, I made a point to talk to her at each class. As a result, she was nearly always prepared.

We teach in the way we prefer to learn. A teacher who prefers the auditory mode of sensory perception often lectures and encourages verbal discussion. The environment in the group lessons tends to be noisy because interaction is encouraged and there is a flurry of activity with students chatting. Skills stressed are playing by ear, ear training, and listening to music.

A teacher who prefers visual perception has an organized studio with attractive displays of posters, pictures, many musical games, and perhaps a staff on the floor and on the board. This teacher prefers that students sit at the piano the entire lesson and motivates them with visually attractive publications.

A teacher preferring the kinesthetic mode often has a large studio with a cluttered desk and piano. She likes students to clap, tap, and dance to rhythms. She may move students away from the piano to act out the mood of a piece or dance a mazurka.

No modality preference is better than another for teaching. In fact, utilizing all modalities, not just the teacher's preference, will enhance the lesson for each student. When a student doesn't understand the first explanation of a new concept, the teacher may adjust her style to accommodate the student's preferred modality. Helping students develop their potential and think creatively requires that teachers actively involve students in the learning process. Modality awareness can help teachers fully engage students in the learning process.

A very reliable source for modality testing is the Swassing-Barbe Modality Index, published in 1979. The Modality Index is a hands-on test and requires no writing. It asks students to identify a progressively complex order of shapes of squares, triangles, and circles. The patterns are given three times, first visually, then aurally, and last kinesthetically. It is appropriate for all ages and takes about twenty minutes to give each student (Modality Index, Barbe and Swassing).

Each of the modalities represents a distinct way of perceiving and learning. Becoming aware of modality strengths and building on a student's strength is a positive approach to music education that is much more effective and efficient than correcting mistakes.

Personality Type. The Myers Briggs Type Indicator is an approach to understanding how we learn. Carl Jung first developed type theory. Then Isabel Myers and her mother, Katherine Briggs, devised a questionnaire that gives insight into the role of personality in influencing human behavior. Although this test is administered by a health professional, various authors have developed similar personality tests. Most are designed for adults, but a few are appropriate for elementary age with types compared to various colors or animals.

Type theory provides a practical tool for understanding students' learning styles. No one type is considered better than another; the theory simply highlights the intriguing differences of each student. Briggs Myers identifies four dimensions of personality types (1–9) (see Fig. 8.2).

The extraversion-introversion preference contrasts students who prefer to be with people to those who are more at ease by themselves. The extravert prefers the outside environment of people and things, and the introvert prefers the inner world of concepts and ideas. Extraverted students like class discussion and group projects and enjoy bouncing ideas off their peers. They understand the

Figure 8.2. Personality Type Dimensions

Ways of dealing with the outer and inner worlds: EI preference	Extraversion	E
	Introversion	I
Ways of perceiving: SN preference	Sensing	S
	Intuition	N
Ways of making decisions: TF preference	Thinking	T
	Feeling	F
Attitude taken toward the outer world: JP preference	Judging	J
	Perceiving	P

subject matter better by talking to others. Although "extroversion" is the usual spelling, Myers Briggs uses "extraversion."

Introverts prefer lectures and reflective tasks, such as reading and writing, to help them assimilate ideas presented in a lesson. A class discussion will often end up with only the extraverts engaging in conversation. Divide the class into small groups of three or four students to encourage the introverts to share their thoughtful ideas.

The sensing-intuition preference reveals major differences in learning styles. Students who prefer sensing perception learn by doing. The sensing personality needs to experience ideas through the senses. For piano students, this means participating at the keyboard and exploring music by playing, hearing, and seeing. They like the reward: a good grade on the test or a prize for doing well. They enjoy the moment, the here-and-now. They rely on experience rather than theory, and trust the customary ways of doing things.

By contrast, students who prefer intuitive perception rely on inspiration rather than past experience. They like abstract theory and the world of ideas. They are energized by the possibilities of an idea, and they instigate new projects. New ways of doing things and creative projects are a welcome challenge. They may have trouble following through with their ideas because they may become overwhelmed with too many ideas and too much to do. They may need help in setting priorities and scheduling their time in order to be productive. Projects that encourage creativity rather than following a set pattern enable the intuitive to flourish.

The thinking-feeling dimension highlights differences in the way that people make decisions. Those who prefer thinking tend to make logical decisions in an impersonal manner. Instruction that is sequential with well-organized materials helps these students. By contrast, students who prefer feeling make decisions based on personal feeling. They consider how their decisions will affect themselves and others. EF types need to have a more personal relationship with the teacher. They work well for a teacher who cares about them and is generous with positive comments. They are keenly aware of the unspoken feeling-tone of the lesson. Each person uses both processes but prefers one to the other.

Finally, the judging-perceiving dimension determines the work habits of a student. Those preferring judging are quick to reach decisions and are not likely to reconsider. Students who favor the perceiving preference consider many possibilities and leave decisions until the last possible moment. They are interested in surveying all the data and possible options rather than finishing the work or making the decision. The judging student will have assignments finished by the deadline or before, but the perceiving student will start the assignment just prior to the deadline and may turn it in late.

Matching Types. One way to utilize this information is to match students' types to particular learning settings, thereby maximizing strengths yet improving on their weaknesses. For instance, the ENFP types (extravert, intuitive, feeling, perceptive) may enjoy group lessons because of the stimulation they get from other people. They seek a caring relationship with the teacher and prefer choices in their assignments so they can use their imagination. They also need help in organizing their practice. Linda, a student teacher in my piano pedagogy class, is an INFP and delights her student, Aaron, with creative activities in his piano lesson. She was puzzled as to why Aaron, an ENFP, did not practice at home. Although he had plenty of stimulation for creativity from his lessons, he did not know how to organize his practice. Linda needed to help him develop a routine and practice the routine at the lesson. Although routine is not the preference of this type, Linda's awareness of this need will allow her the flexibility to approach practice in an organized manner.

Common Types. Seventy percent of the student population are extraverts, according to Myers's research, and 70 percent prefer sensory perception (Lawrence 39). Therefore, school classrooms and piano studios should gear instruction so that this 70 percent can talk to others and have hands-on experiences. On the contrary, most instructors use lectures and solitary assignments, which are geared to the other 30 percent. The most common type is ESTJ (extravert, sensing, thinking, judging). The least common type is INFP (introvert, intuition, feeling, perceiving).

There are sixteen possible combinations using the four preferences. Figure 8.3 identifies the sixteen types and characteristics of each type.

Type Teaching Examples. Following are examples of personality types gleaned from student-teachers' thoughts about their students' lessons. They grappled with adapting their instruction to help students who were different types from themselves.

Andrea, ISFJ (introvert, sensing, feeling, judging), likes order in her classroom with a minimum of noise. She realized the importance of allowing extraverts to talk to one another during piano class. Her group of college-age beginners began the semester listening to her lecture and then practicing alone using

Figure 8.3. Sixteen Combinations of the Four Preferences: EI SN TF JP

ISTJ	ISFJ	INFJ	INTJ
Organized and methodical. Likes hands-on activities. Quiet, opinionated, and quick to make decisions.	Friendly. Dependable. Likes routine. Likes to please. Would rather try it than hear about it. Loyal and conscientious.	Likes to work alone. Creative and sensitive. Well-respected and takes responsibility. Has close friends. Gets things done.	Creative, disciplined. Pursues interests enthusiastically. Independent, critical, determined, stubborn.
ISTP	ISFP	INFP	INTP
Observant, quiet, reserved. Has to be interested in the subject to do well. Does just enough to get by; any more is a waste of energy.	Quiet, modest, retiring. Loyal follower. Enjoys the present and rather relaxed about getting things done. Doesn't like disagreements.	Enthusiastic and loyal. Conscientious to a fault. Likes to learn and try new things. Tends to be disorganized and does too much, but gets it done.	Quiet and reserved. Enjoys reading, thinking of possibilities. Tends to put off finishing projects that are not of interest.
ESTP	ESFP	ENFP	ENTP
Easy-going. Likes whatever comes along. Conservative. Very accomplished, but may take on more at the expense of quality.	Friendly, easy-going, enjoys life and makes it fun for those around him. Prefers learning facts rather than theories. Common sense. Ability to work with people.	Enthusiastic, inventive. Enjoys people, which energizes her. Needs encouragement to feel comfortable. Tends to procrastinate and "wing it" rather than preparing.	Resourceful, logical, intelligent, good at many things. May neglect the routine. Enjoyable company. Likes to play the devil's advocate.
ESTJ	ESFJ	ENFJ	ENTJ
Realistic and matter-of-fact. Impatient if not interested in the subject. Likes to organize and run things. May have to be reminded to consider others' feelings.	Popular, talkative, good humor. The life of the party or meeting. Works best with encouragement. Doesn't like abstract thinking. Wants to nobly affect people.	High achiever. Conscientious, good leader, sensitive, creative. Concerned with what others think. Sociable, popular, and sympathetic.	Talkative, blunt, takes leadership. Good public speaker. Reasons well and well-informed. Overconfident to a fault.

headphones in a digital piano laboratory. However, the students didn't practice what they were assigned or didn't practice at all. Andrea divided the class into small groups of like ability and had them practice together. The piano lab controller allows students to hear one another through the headphones. They played scales for each other, improved their sight reading significantly because they were forced to concentrate, and enjoyed improvising duets. The teacher achieved her goals for the group by adjusting her teaching style to theirs. Most of the students were extraverts and they were much more productive when they practiced together.

Stephanie describes her exuberant personality type, INFJ (introvert, intuitive, feeling, judging), and her struggle to adjust to Megan's quiet, studious type:

> The energy I usually have while teaching had to be stifled somewhat when working with Megan. She is much quieter and intimidated when I get rowdy. She often plays with a shy and timid sound because she is afraid of making mistakes. I wanted her to be more comfortable making mistakes, and to play with conviction. Music is such a fun activity, I wanted her to be happy at whatever she might create, mistakes and all. Working with duets where I purposefully overpower her, and she realizes she has

the melody, brings out more sound in her. Megan has taught me that I do not always have to be overtly happy and giddy. Even though she may not be joining in on all my clapping, singing, or other movements, she is observing what I do and digesting its meaning. She has made me more aware that I must congratulate students often on their accomplishments, so they feel competent to progress to the next level. When I praise her, her sound becomes full of life.

Piano Pedagogy Student Types. Over the past several years, nearly 150 piano pedagogy students at Wichita State University have taken the R. Craig Hogan and David Champagne "Personal Style Inventory" assessment. Records were kept on ninety of those students. A large majority of the students are introverts (67 percent) with an equal distribution perceiving by intuition or sensing. An overwhelming percentage make decisions by feeling versus thinking (76 percent). Most of the students approach their outer worlds through judging (70 percent). The most frequent types, forty-seven out of ninety, were nearly equally divided between ISFJ, INFJ, INFP, and ESFJ. Thus among these students introversion, feeling, and judging are preferred, and intuition and sensing preferences are equally divided.

The distribution of the piano pedagogy students' personality types does not agree with the population at large. Sixty-seven percent of the students are introverts, whereas a majority of the population at large are extraverts—72 percent. The largest type category in the piano pedagogy group is NF (intuitive, feeling); whereas the majority of the population at large is ST (sensing, thinking). Intuitive-feeling types are said to be suited to occupations such as author, journalist, and pedagogue. The music teaching profession is a creative occupation as are the above professions. One-third of the piano pedagogy students prefer sensing and feeling. Occupations for SF types tend to be as artists, entertainers, vendors, and conservators.

My type, ENFP (extravert, intuitive, feeling, perceiving), is different in three of the four dimensions from a majority of the piano pedagogy students that I teach. I have adapted the course materials and my method of teaching the class to accommodate their learning styles. For instance, as 70 percent prefer judging, which means they like organization and getting things done, I provide a detailed syllabus of assignments for the semester. Reading and project assignments are listed with due dates. This is difficult for me because I prefer to keep assignments open-ended and let one class lead to another as interests dictate. I also force myself to write the assignment on the board for the students to see. My preference is to give the assignment verbally. My struggle in writing on the board is evident in its sloppy and disorganized appearance.

Another difference between the students and me is my insistence on class discussion. Because nearly 70 percent of the students are introverts, they prefer to work alone and think about issues rather than talk about them. I want them to share ideas and different perceptions. A compromise that has worked well through the years is to subgroup the students into groups of three or four. After they discuss the issue for five or ten minutes, a spokesperson for the group will share their ideas.

The pedagogy students teach a group of young children together, and those not teaching are observing. Since there are about three times more observers than teachers and students, the pedagogy students team-teach the class. Observing other introverts as well as the two or three extraverts teach the class eases their inhibitions of being "on stage" and gives them many ideas to develop their teaching style.

Finally, we have one preference alike! Nearly 70 percent of my students are feeling types. I can empathize with them on this point. We need to feel appreciated and encouraged for the work we do. I respond to them in a positive manner and balance my criticisms of their work with comments about what they do well.

Each student is a valuable asset to the class, which I reflect in my interaction with them. One problem issue is that feeling types may make decisions intended to please one another rather than risk conflict. However, conflict of opinions is necessary for intellectual and emotional growth. If the environment supports this growth, the class will progress beyond the "honeymoon stage," where they like one another because of their similarities, to a stage where they appreciate their individual differences.

Perhaps there is an explanation for why students who are introverts (70 percent) choose to become piano majors. An introvert prefers or at least tolerates practicing piano for many hours in a room alone. Extraverts would rather be interacting with people. As an extravert, my career preferences are teaching piano and playing chamber music because I can interact with others.

Seventy percent of the students in my class are feeling types. Performing music demands projection of the emotional content of the music. Identifying with the music emotionally as well as intellectually enables one to perform expressively. It is not a surprise, therefore, that such a high percentage of piano majors would be feeling types.

Perhaps piano pedagogy students prefer judging (70 percent) because musicians have to make quick decisions on the spot as to how the music will go. Practice entails constant assessment and making choices between a variety of interpretations. Judging types can concentrate on a project for a long time, which is a necessity for practicing the piano.

Yes, musicians are different. The most common type in the population is ESTJ (extravert, sensing, thinking, judging), and most of the pianists in my class differ on two out of four of those dimensions. We have always said that people in other fields don't understand artists. It's no surprise to us that we really do perceive and think differently.

Student-Teacher Comments. In the following paragraphs I discuss four student-teachers who have common personality types of the WSU piano majors. They wrote papers for me about their teaching and their words reveal the particular characteristics of their type.

Anthony's personality type is ISTJ (introvert, sensing, thinking, judging). His plans for a non-major piano class illustrate the type's concern for organization and specificity. Anthony praises the text's methodical approach and plans to finish Chapter 6 by midterm, and the whole book by the end of the semester. He vows ambitiously that the students will be able to play six pieces by ear with basic harmony and all five-finger major and minor scales by midterm, and twelve pieces by ear along with all one-octave major scales by the end of the semester.

Anthony sums up his strengths: "My natural tendencies to be detail-oriented help me to be a good problem solver with students one-on-one. I like to analyze problems in a commonsense way and try to come up with ways to solve them." Anthony's comments about analyzing problems and being detailed-oriented are typical of persons of this type. He continues, "As a student myself, I have always preferred taking classes where the professor just lectured and I could take notes, deciding what I needed to retain, and what I could ignore. And I learn well that way. I liked finding a quiet spot later by myself where I could devour my notes and figure out what the key points were that the professor made. Plus I know that the majority of people learn in a much different way than I do—thriving on interaction and activity."

Anthony's observations about the class at the end of the semester are much less specific, and he conceded that they were having difficulty achieving his ambitious goals by midterm. By this time he had forgotten the goal of all major scales by semester's end along with twelve tunes by ear and instead was very pleased with the students' ability to learn the white key majors plus C sharp and F sharp along with completing the text. Most remarkable in Anthony's teaching was his awareness that the students do not learn as he does, and he was able to begin adapting his teaching style to their preferences. He experienced that lecturing too much can stymie a group. He describes what happened. "Josh was turned off by my teaching approach and would resort to doodling around on his keyboard while I lectured, jumping from one topic to the next. I think this kind of teaching sort of desensitizes the student—maybe even makes them feel less than human, not an individual. By teaching in this way, one is basically giving the message that the student's role in the class is to sit, be quiet, and listen. This is obviously destructive when the goal is to get students to be a productive part of the learning that is going on."

Alicia, an ISFJ type (introverted, sensing, feeling, judging), said it was a revelation to her to see how different each person really is, and added that it has helped her teaching to realize they may not perceive as she does. Alicia is a very gifted teacher. When she was only twenty her student won the high school division of a local scholarship contest. Her students play with much flair and poise. She is very conscientious about providing me with lesson plans, self-evaluations, and videos of her students every week of the semester. She says she would like to spend more time on improvisation, sight reading, and ear training, "although in general, the students don't want to focus on these areas! They'd rather be learning impressive, showy repertoire!" The SFJ type likes to play the

impressive repertoire and tends to put technical exercises on the back burner. I think Alicia thrives on teaching the "showy repertoire" and getting her students to play the music well.

Alicia talks about two of her students who are also her sisters. Casey, a seven-year-old, learns by watching and listening and has trouble sitting still and concentrating for very long. Alicia says Casey taught her to be flexible rather than stick with her pre-planned goals. When Casey was distracted or fidgety, or was excited about a piece she had figured out, Alicia discovered that they would get more accomplished if she listened to her rather than ignoring her behavior and going on with her agenda. At the beginning of the semester, Alicia complained about the lack of motivation of her fourteen-year-old sister, Lauren, even though she is very musical. Alicia worked to change her perception of Lauren from "little sister" to treating her as an adult. She says, "Some of our best discussions during lessons were when we became music colleagues and forgot about the fact that we were still teacher and student. She had some great musical ideas to share!" I think Lauren also may be an ISFJ and is achievement motivated. She accomplished an incredible amount during the semester, passing two levels of the state music progression tests, and learning and performing some favorite pieces from the repertoire: Chopin's Polonaise in A major, Beethoven's "Marcia Alla Turca," Debussy's "Clair de Lune," Mozart's "Rondo alla Turca," Copland's "Cat and Mouse," and selections from Mendelssohn's *Song Without Words*. She excelled at playing four-octave scales and arpeggios.

Stephanie, an INFJ type (introverted, intuitive, feeling, judging), describes her strength in teaching as her dedication and love of music. She adds, "I can only hope the children see this and respect it and look to me for direction." She is well respected by her peers and teachers. She has received many awards for her outstanding performance and academic excellence. Although she prefers to work alone, she is a very responsible member of the collegiate music teachers' organization and often volunteers for projects and gets them done.

Stephanie's well-written description of each of her students in a piano class of six-year-olds is typical of her keen perception of others. "Brandon seems very quick and very pleasant. I want to be sure he feels like he fits in since he is the only boy. Makayla is a very sweet girl, but has already been accused of pushing in the first class. I have to pay close attention to see who the real culprit is. Rachel is very quiet, but so nice. I already am very fond of her, because she never speaks unless answering a question and seems very into learning" (Rachel sounds most like Stephanie.) "Taylor is very much in need of constant attention. She had a little encounter with Makayla and really blew it out of proportion. She may be the most difficult to handle."

Andrea, an ESFJ type (extravert, sensing, feeling, judging), was extremely frustrated with her first experience of teaching a piano class. The students in the class were divided equally between two levels of curriculum. Beginners were in one group, while the other had students who had studied piano for one semester or longer. Andrea's comments about her strengths and weaknesses illustrate her type's concerns. She had worked with the class for about six weeks.

> I am usually pretty aware of what each student's problem is, but I'm finding it hard to help everyone during each class period. Sometimes I think my help isn't very productive because I'm helping so many people in a limited amount of time. There are other times when I spend too much time with a problem, so I just need to learn how to balance this out. I feel like I have a positive relationship with my class, but I need to make sure that I treat everyone equally. I'm learning that it is very easy to let students feel left out without even realizing it. It is very difficult to get the quiet students to ask questions. Another strength that I have is that I tend to ask questions while I am explaining a new concept or reviewing an old one. This way the students are beginning to apply what they are learning instead of just listening.

By the end of the semester Andrea settled into a routine of small group activities where students discussed concepts with each other and played together. She divided her time equally between the groups. My written evaluations of her teaching, encouraging her by pointing out what she did well, coaxed her to hang in there and keep trying.

An awareness of personality types and the modalities of visual, auditory, and kinesthetic can open up new approaches for the teacher. Adapting instruction to individual learning styles has limitless possibilities for assisting teachers in developing the individual's highest potential. Ultimately, whatever helps us communicate the joy of music has value.

Suggested Reading

Barbe and Swassing, *Teaching through Modality Strengths.*
Golay, *Learning Patterns and Temperament Styles.*
Keirsey and Bates, *Please Understand Me.*
Lawrence, *People Types and Tiger Stripes: A Practical Guide to Learning Styles.*
Myers and Myers, *Gifts Differing.*
"Pedagogy Saturday VI, Exploring Learning Styles: Developing a Flexible Teaching Approach."

Further Thought

• What is your personality type and modality?
• How will awareness of personality types and modalities affect your teaching?

- Suggest teaching strategies to adapt to students' modality preferences—visual, auditory, kinesthetic.
- Suggest teaching strategies to adapt to each personality type dimension.
  - Extraversion or introversion
  - Sensing or intuition
  - Thinking or feeling
  - Judging or perceiving

9 Introduction to Group Teaching

With the increased popularity of group lessons during the past century, the teacher has become a group leader, not only for providing inspiration about music and performance but also for the ability to motivate participation and stimulate group morale. Teachers have found that they need help in guiding students to acquire skills of leadership, cooperation, and responsible membership—principles conducive to productive learning experiences.

Experienced teachers anticipate the pace of the learning experience: how long the transfer student will take to adjust to a new teacher and begin making progress, or how long before a festival or contest the composition should be memorized in order to perform successfully. Likewise, teachers of groups realize that a group of students has its own progression of growth that largely influences the progress of each student. Students in groups want to know what being a member of the group will be like. Will they be allowed to talk or joke, will other students criticize them, will learning be fun, will they progress?

Groups naturally progress through stages of establishing membership, looking to leadership, expressing feelings, respecting individual differences, and, finally, becoming productive. When groups function productively, individuals progress and are more positive about their learning than they are when learning alone. Teachers can influence the progression of the group's growth, and suggestions are given to help facilitate the growth stages of groups (Chapter 10).

One factor important to effective group teaching is placement of students into homogeneous groups based on age and ability so that members can learn from one another. Inevitably a student may progress more quickly or slowly than other students. Groups are fluid and in a constant state of evolving. Students who have been grouped well will most likely progress in a natural manner. If they do not progress, however, it may be necessary to regroup or place a student in individual lessons (Chapter 9).

Often the first question from teachers who are new to group teaching is "How do you keep each student involved while one is playing?" Additional questions arise such as, Do they all play the same music? Can they have solos that aren't the same? How do you teach if the students are using different method books? These questions are mostly about music materials. More important issues pertain to guiding students to understand musical concepts and principles that will enable them to play a variety of music and become competent in a variety of skills. Such musical competency will equip students to enjoy music for a lifetime (Chapter 11).

Finally, in cooperative learning environments teachers have a new role—that of facilitator. Many viable opinions arise in group lessons, and the teacher's task is to facilitate the lesson so that students grow musically, intellectually, and socially. Fortunately, experts in cognitive theory and group dynamics can assist the group piano teacher (Chapter 12).

Teachers may be overwhelmed with the demands of group teaching. However, the hours of study and planning are well worth it when lessons are energetic, musical, and filled with student insights into music. Application of these principles of grouping, group development, problem solving, and group dynamics will lead to effective group teaching.

Assigning Students to Groups

In order for students to learn from one another and evolve into productive groups, placement by age and ability is most important. In addition, awareness of students' strengths and weaknesses, as well as learning styles, can determine which students will work well as a group.

What do you do in a group when one student learns quickly and another learns slowly, when one is prepared and one is not? Tom, a graduate student-teacher, reflected on this problem in his first month of teaching class piano:

> Sometimes I don't know if I should wait for those who learn slowly, or go ahead with those who learn quickly. I am still not sure about their theory levels, so sometimes I have trouble knowing when to explain theory carefully or just mention it. Sometimes when the class is playing together, there are always some students who can find the right position quickly while others are still wondering. I don't know if I should wait for everyone to find their position or begin when most of them are ready. Some concepts seem to be very easy for some students, but maybe very difficult for others. What is the best way to handle this?

Tom is aware of very real issues in the college piano class. The students in Tom's class are freshmen music majors and have had little or no previous piano lessons. After he gains experience in observing each student's capabilities, questions will be answered about introducing theory topics, knowing when all are ready for the downbeat, and presenting concepts in a way that challenges students' thinking yet clarifies their understanding.

Young teachers are usually so focused on what to teach that they are not always aware of how the student is responding internally as well as externally. A student may have good theoretical understanding, but have difficulty coordinating both hands together. Another student may have good facility yet not understand the form and structure of the composition. These students are probably well grouped because they have varying strengths and weaknesses and therefore can benefit from each other's viewpoints.

In teaching the transfer student, the teacher has expectations about what the student should know. The student may be transferring from another teacher or another section of a college piano class. The teacher presumes that the new student knows the basics of note reading and rhythm if she has studied for one or two years. If she is in the second level, the teacher presumes that she is proficient with the first level of a college piano proficiency curriculum. Never presume! Teachers can be unnecessarily disappointed and students can be mistakenly labeled as slow or fast.

Thus an audition is needed for each student in order to evaluate strengths and weaknesses. Then, after becoming familiar with the student's background, proceed to help the student improve. A pet peeve of mine is teachers' complaints about transfer students' poor musical background, an implication that the previous teacher was not effective. Placing blame doesn't help the student to improve.

Assess the present capabilities of the student and plan strategies for progress in order to set a positive direction for future lessons. Always interview transfer students to determine their background, especially if the student will join a group lesson. Hear them play a piece of their choice and ask them to sight read. Test aural skills in rhythm, pitch range, direction and intervals, scale and technique skills, and reading skills. For aural testing have the child clap back rhythms that the teacher claps, then have him sing and play an easy melody by ear. To evaluate the student's understanding of key signatures as well as hand position, posture, and facility, ask the child to play major and minor scales and chord progressions.

The beginning student also should be auditioned. The session will be an introduction to music study as well as a readiness test of pitch and rhythmic aural skills (Table 9.1). The session can reassure students and parents that music study will be a positive experience.

Test rhythm perception with clap backs of short rhythmic patterns. Assess pitch discrimination by playing two notes and asking the child to decide if the second pitch is higher or lower. Have the child sing a well-known tune with you such as "Jingle Bells," and assess if he is able to continue singing without your help. Check technical ability by placing the child's hands over a five-finger position. Assess the child's ease first in playing hands alone, then in contrary and parallel motion. Ask the student questions about favorite songs, activities, and subjects to get to know him. Ask the parents if they own a piano and their intentions for encouraging practice.

Music majors enrolled in college piano proficiency classes should be placed in sections that are compatible with their piano background and ability. Students can be interviewed and auditioned during freshman and transfer student orientation programs or prior to the first week of classes. Design the audition to test skills that will be covered during the first semester of study. Assure students that the test is only for placement in a homogeneous section. For students with no background up to three years of background, assess theory and technique by modeling a scale and chord progression. Those with no background may be able to imitate well and those with some background may play with ease. To assess reading ability have students sight read at a level of difficulty required at the end of a semester of study. Give the audition in groups of two to four students with the first playing as a rehearsal together, and with the second as an individual test for scoring. Students with four to ten years of background can

Table 9.1. Audition Test for Children

Circle a number (5 being most proficient) that correlates with the student's abilities. Make note of the child's responsiveness and attitude.

1. Rhythm discrimination

Clap the patterns twice. Ask student to repeat.

1 2 3 4 5

1 2 3 4 5

2. Pitch discrimination

Tell student you will be playing two notes. Ask student to answer which note is higher, the first or second note.

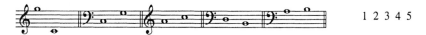

1 2 3 4 5

Ask the student to sing "Jingle Bells" with you and assess intonation and independence.

1 2 3 4 5

3. Technical ease

Place student's hands over a five-finger scale on C. Model each step of playing.

Hands alone	1 2 3 4 5
Hands in contrary motion	1 2 3 4 5
Hands in parallel motion	1 2 3 4 5

4. Note and rhythm reading

If the student has had prior lessons assess sight reading ability.   1 2 3 4 5

be directed to play a scale and chord progression without modeling, read a four-part chorale, and harmonize and transpose a melody (Table 9.2).

Usually universities provide digital piano classrooms with multiple pianos. For larger music programs with several classes offered, designate sections for students with more background as well as beginning classes. For smaller music

Table 9.2. Audition Test for College Music Majors

Note to teacher: Play and show the cadence twice before they play. Have the group play the skill once together and then score the individual playing. The sight reading example may be played out of range if more than one person are at a piano. Ask students if they have had formal instruction, and if so, for how long.

Form groups of four students according to their background.
 No background
 One to three years of background
 Four to ten years of background
 Piano majors

Audition for students with no background
 1. Scale: D major, hands separately (play for them twice)
 2. Cadence: D major—I–IV$_4^6$–I–V$_5^6$–I—hands separately (play for them twice).
 3. Sight read: Level I example, hands together (assure students that they will be able to play easily a piece of similar difficulty by the end of the first semester of study).

Audition for students with one to three years of background
 1. Scale: D major, hands separately
 2. Cadence: D major—I–IV–I–V^7–I—(RH I^6 chord; LH root) (play for them twice).
 3. Sight read: Level two example

Audition for students with four or more years of background and piano majors
 1. Scale: D major, hands together; E harmonic minor, hands together (do not play for them).
 2. Cadence: D major—I–IV–V^7/V–V^7–I—(RH I^6; LH roots) (play for them twice).
 3. Sight read: four-part chorale

programs, students may be subgrouped according to ability into groups of four or less. Subgrouping is most important in large classes of twelve to twenty-four. Chapter 12 suggests strategies to encourage effective group dynamics by occasionally dividing large classes into small groups of two to four students.

If students have been grouped properly, progress will be swift and students will learn from one another. In the first class, assess their understanding and facility by designing a lesson that includes a scale and chord, playing by ear, harmonizing, transposing, improvising, and reading. The following design has been used with college classes for individual assessment of both beginners and piano majors. Ask a teaching assistant to help with scoring each skill while you direct the playing. This is an assessment activity, so refrain from instructing. The order of each activity will be as follows:

• Model what is to be played.
• Direct students to play once together for practice.
• Direct students to play individually without stopping between students.

Encourage continuity in playing by conducting, counting, or accompanying. Score the individual playing on a scale from one to four, with four being highest. The assessment activity gives the teacher information about each student's ability and gives the class an overview of the functional skills to be learned.

Suggested Reading

Baker-Jordan, *Practical Piano Pedagogy.*
Bastien, *How to Teach Piano Successfully.*
"Getting Started in Group Teaching."
Gigante, *A Business Guide for the Music Teacher.*
"One-on-One and Three-or-More Teaching."
Piano Pedagogy Forum, <http://music.sc.edu/ea/keyboard/ppf/>.
Pianonet, National Piano Foundation, <http://pianonet.com/>.
"Three or More Teaching."
Uszler et al., *The Well-Tempered Keyboard Teacher.*

Further Thought

- What are advantages of teaching in groups?
- What are disadvantages of teaching in groups?
- Why is good grouping important?
- Suggest ways to test a beginning student's rhythmic, melodic, and technical abilities in an audition.
- What factors would you consider in grouping students in order to learn from one another?

10 Group Growth

We join a group of people to achieve a goal that is important to us. The group may be a class required for a degree, a committee for planning and making decisions for a larger unit, a board for running an organization, or a group lesson for learning to play the piano. We bring to the group different experiences, points of view, and expectations. Every group goes through a growth pattern that may be described as a progression from initial questions about membership in the group to the last stage of productivity where problems are solved effectively. According to Guy Duckworth, a group's productivity is determined by the successful progression through each of five stages of growth: membership, influence, feelings, individual differences, and productivity.* After membership issues are resolved, the group deals with leadership questions, progresses to trusting relationships so that feelings are shared openly, and finally individual differences are respected in achieving a deeper understanding of the issues (Table 10.1).

Upon attending the first group lesson, students wonder if the lesson will be fun or serious, challenging or boring. Will it be okay to come late or miss class? Will the atmosphere be formal or relaxed? Will students be able to express opinions and play without fear of ridicule and embarrassment? Will it be okay to make mistakes? Teachers provide guidance through the membership stage by giving students long-term and short-term objectives. A lecture about the curriculum, reinforced by a written syllabus or a studio policy, gives students a general idea of the teacher's expectations and what they will be playing and learning. Rules of conduct should be established in the initial lessons by the teacher, or together with the students, concerning absence, tardiness, care of equipment, and respect for others' playing and talking. The teacher indirectly communicates the style of interaction to be expected through lectures and directions about the lessons, and through questions and conversations in getting to know the students.

As questions of membership are answered for each student, the group turns to the issue of influence. Who is the leader of this group? Will the teacher share the leadership role with the students? How will members influence one another? Do they have similar interests? Will they like one another? Will they be supportive or competitive? Will anyone try to dominate the others? Groups in which the teacher shares the leadership role are more likely to progress to later stages of growth. Teachers facilitate this growth by recognizing the strengths

---

*I am indebted to Dr. Guy Duckworth, a leading expert in the field of group piano and my professor at the University of Colorado, for teaching me about patterns of group growth and group dynamics.

Table 10.1

Stages of Group Growth
1. Membership
2. Influence
3. Feelings
4. Individual differences
5. Productivity

and weaknesses of each individual and encouraging students to learn from each other. Inviting students to make decisions assures them that they are capable of leadership. Students can choose the tempo in a duet or assign a scale for a group member to play. Encouraging students to cooperate with one another rather than compete helps guide students to later stages of growth.

Progress to the next stage is evident if group members express feelings openly in the lesson rather than waiting until they are out the door to whisper their feelings to one another. When students express feelings to one another as well as the teacher, this is a signal to the teacher that the group is progressing well: students feel that they are valued in the group and that their contributions won't be ignored or belittled. It is very difficult for a teacher to be aware of the feelings of four to twelve or more students at a time. Not only is it important to listen and accept expressed feelings, teachers also have to be aware of unspoken feelings that are expressed through body language and attitudes. What is the student really saying when he acts up in class or is not responsive? Reading between the lines and asking students to express their feelings is vital to the group for reaching the objectives of the lesson.

The next stage deals with individual differences. Prior to this stage, students have grown to like one another because of their similarities. In this stage, the "honeymoon" is over and students learn how to deal with people different from themselves. Will it be okay to express an opinion that is different from others' opinions? How will others react when opinions and ideas conflict? Will they be "blacklisted" and no longer included in the group because they disagree? Will their ideas be respected? Can group members discuss and argue their opinions without fear of group censure? Often the most lasting change comes from conflict. When a group member disagrees with another, the leader encourages both sides to explain their views so that new understandings and solutions to the problem can be found.

The last stage of productivity occurs when groups have effectively dealt with the issues of membership, influence, feelings, and individual differences. Students actively discuss and experiment with problems and come up with productive solutions. Each student's learning is enhanced by the group's work on lesson objectives such as polishing a contest piece or a duet for performance, learning minor scales, or improving sight reading.

Following is a graduate student's discussion of the stages of group growth in a proficiency class for college piano majors. Most of her discussion deals with the portion of class devoted to sight reading and ensemble playing.

> It is exciting to have discovered they have moved through the five dimensions of the student role in a group. These five dimensions include: membership, influence, feelings, individual differences, and productivity. The first three lessons were at the *membership* stage. The students were learning how to interact with me, the teacher, and with each other in a slightly different environment than last semester. The students really opened up when experiencing eurhythmics. In discussing Romantic characteristics, I asked the class how we could play the Schubert piece "Allegro Moderato" more musically. Kyle suggested dancing. It was a great idea and so I involved the whole class in dancing to the music. Everyone was surprised, but participated and really enjoyed it. It was one of the exciting moments of teaching. The students immediately played the piece more musically after dancing! I think at this point they realized that membership in this class would be exciting, participatory, and would contain an open atmosphere for questions and learning.
>
> This lesson also introduced the next stage of the student role—*influence*. Kyle's suggestion of dancing was not mocked or shoved aside. I tried it and this let him and the others know that they had influence in the class. It let them know that anyone could be a leader or have a good idea. This stage continued through to the next week's lesson when Angela took the lead during the rehearsal of the Debussy piece. She had worked on the piano solo portion and had some good suggestions for the class. I listened to her comments and used them to structure the rehearsal and address problems that she defined.
>
> The class moved into the third stage of the student role in this lesson—*feelings*. Eric made the comment that he didn't like sight reading. I wasn't sure how to respond. I now know that I should have accepted his feeling by simply saying, "Yes, it is hard." Sarah also commented that sight reading was hard. They felt free to discuss their feelings about sight reading and give helpful tips and comments.
>
> At the midterm lesson we passed into the fourth phase of student role—*individual differences*. The students shared their experience of Bartók's *Mikrokosmos* pieces that they had prepared for the midterm. Everyone learned some valuable information and from many different points of view. I felt this was a much more interesting way to learn about Bartók's music than coming from one source—the teacher. Not everyone

agreed about their feelings for contemporary music. Not everyone saw Bartók in the same light. Despite these differences they seemed to appreciate each other's viewpoints and came away learning more than they would have by themselves.

I'm not exactly sure when the last stage, *productivity,* fully developed. Becky's suggestion on changing the counting was an obvious sign that we had reached this goal. Becky asked a question about changing the counting in the Debussy piece, *En Bateau,* to six beats instead of a compound two. She felt it might improve the accuracy of the entrance. This showed that she was thinking independently and felt free to make this suggestion. We tried her idea and it was definitely more successful than what we were doing before. This was an exciting moment to discover that we had reached the productivity stage together as a class.

In the membership stage, the teacher recognized that students had to adjust to interacting with her and with each other in a somewhat different way than they had in the previous semester with another teacher. She appreciated their previous background and realized the change would take some adjustment. A turning point in the group's growth occurred when a student made a suggestion and the teacher used the idea. In response to her question, "How can we play Schubert more musically?" Kyle suggested dancing the piece. The teacher accepted his idea and used it. She had the class dance to feel the meter of the piece. She went out on a limb, not only by directing college students to get off the bench and dance, but because she had not had much experience with dancing. She did understand the importance of using students' ideas and had studied eurhythmics in pedagogy class. Her flexibility allowed the group to experience a new way of working together with the result of a better performance and sheer enjoyment.

The teacher indirectly told class members they could influence the class direction when she accepted Kyle's recommendation to dance. Because of the teacher's encouragement of student leadership, Becky did not hesitate at the next class to give her ideas about the Debussy duet she had been practicing. Becky's ideas were used to structure the rehearsal on the Debussy. By building on the student's ideas, the teacher reinforced the atmosphere that students should practice, think of ideas to contribute, and express them in class.

The next stage of feelings was encouraged by the teacher through questions about their strengths and weaknesses as sight readers and by her acceptance of those feelings that were heartfelt. The class was a mixture of excellent, average, and poor sight readers. The teacher allowed students to express feelings and chided herself for not verbally acknowledging the student who felt that sight reading is hard. Other students responded by sharing ideas for sight reading. The teacher did not interfere and allowed this discussion to happen. Sometimes teachers have to get out of the way for students to learn.

In the last rehearsal before an ensemble concert, students were intensely involved in their practice for the concert and Angela suggested ways to perfect the performance. Their motivation to play well in the concert caused them to offer complex solutions to polish the duet. The teacher is to be commended for committing herself to the process of learning at this final rehearsal, rather than reversing her established way of participatory leadership and becoming the dictator.

We can expect a class of young adults with extensive piano background to be more verbally involved than young children. However, children will experience the same stages in defining their role in the group. Each age group's productivity is determined by the successful progression through the five stages of growth.

Suggested Reading

Duckworth, "Group Lessons for Advanced Students with No Private Lessons," and "Group Dynamics."

Further Thought

- Think of groups of which you are a member (a school class, a piano performance class, an organization, a sports team). Describe what stage of growth each group reached.
- How can you help students feel comfortable and relate to group members?

11 Problem Solving in Group Lessons

The student's exploration of musical concepts is aided by the group setting. In other words, two or more heads are better than one. As music teachers we want to present musical concepts to students in each lesson and develop their skill in playing musically with ease. The ideas of several students give more possibilities for exploring a concept and discovering how to apply the concept. The stages of problem solving—presentation, definition, experimentation, and verification—are discussed in Chapter 3. Here, we will focus on problem solving in groups with suggestions for activities to engage each member. Several group lessons, taught by student-teachers, are evaluated to illustrate the topics discussed.

The teacher's responsibility is to help students define the problem, limit the conditions of the problem, facilitate the exploration of solutions, and provide clues to help solve the problem. Think of the problem to be solved as an objective for the lesson. A lesson may focus on one objective, such as improving a performance, or on several objectives, such as learning a rhythm, a scale, and dynamic contrast. Problems may arise from the student's playing, a student's question, or from the teacher's presentation of a musical concept.

In planning a lesson consider the following to encourage active participation from each student: (1) provide appropriate challenge; (2) plan a direct experience with concepts to be learned; (3) limit conditions to focus on a particular concept; (4) form principles from concepts that can be transferred to other music; (5) transfer concepts to a variety of functional skills; and 6) ask questions to assess student needs and optimize student motivation (Table 11.1).

No matter whether the objectives of the lesson are playing in a method book or improving a performance, plan a conceptual approach rather than a specific one so that all students can be involved in each other's music. Rather than a series of individual lessons correcting each student's mistakes, give a group lesson that challenges students to think about musical concepts.

Emily, a graduate student-teacher, presented the task of composing a short piano piece to her class of elementary-aged students. She limited the composition to one hand using $\frac{3}{4}$ or $\frac{4}{4}$ meter. Because it was the final lesson of the session, she wanted to review all concepts learned. The composition was a hands-on approach to review concepts and was a challenge to each student. She presented the problem by first reviewing clefs, bar line, note values, meter, rests, and dynamics. Then they began the experimentation with the concepts. Emily provided staff paper and directed each compositional step:

1) Decide if you will play in right or left hand and treble or bass clef.
2) Decide $\frac{3}{4}$ or $\frac{4}{4}$ meter.

Table 11.1

Problem-Solving Techniques
1. Challenge
2. Musical concepts
3. Limit conditions
4. Musical principles
5. Functional skills/transfer
6. Motivation

3) Draw bar lines for eight measures with a double bar at the end.
4) Draw rhythm below the staff using different note values.
5) Use a five-finger pattern and put finger numbers below the rhythm.

Emily's plan is a conceptual one and required students to apply what they had learned about singing and playing melodies. They demonstrated their understanding of the concepts by playing the composed piece for class.

Challenge

Effective lessons have the following characteristics: presentations are challenging and success is possible, but not certain; students can use concepts already learned; solutions to the problem will improve the playing; and concepts learned can be compared for similarities or differences to other music and other skills such as transposing. In a group setting the problem selected should challenge each member and build on concepts already learned.

Known to the Unknown. One task in planning a lesson is to select objectives that will ensure that each student can be successful in understanding and using the new concept. Sherry, a graduate student teacher, planned a lesson for five- and six-year-olds to play a tune by ear based on a previous practice procedure they had learned (the known). The students were familiar with clapping and walking the rhythm and shaping the steps, skips, and repeats in the air before playing. The students knew how to play melodies on black keys, but the challenge at this lesson was to learn melodies and note names of white keys on the staff and keyboard (the unknown). Sherry had them complete worksheets identifying C–D–E and G–A–B on the keyboard. Using the familiar practice procedure, they played the song by ear in C position, looked at the song written on a staff, and then transferred what they learned to G position. Thus, the students realized the principle that melodies sound the same starting on different notes if steps, skips, and repeats remain the same.

As the teacher led them in a direct experience to learn the rhythm and melody, she asked questions and encouraged their efforts. They actively participated in learning the song and all felt the responsibility to join in and work hard. The lesson objective of playing by ear and transposing was an appropriate challenge and students were successful because they had played by ear before, but had not transposed. The teacher checked their understanding of the concept of melody by transposing it to G position. They understood that melodic intervals can be transposed to another key and will retain the information since they did it at the lesson.

A teacher listens and reacts to underlying problems in the student's playing in order to give suggestions to improve the playing. At a lesson with two adolescent sisters, Deborah and Angela, Diane told Deborah that she needed to play with more continuity, but gave no clues as to how to do this. They continued to work on the piece but Deborah made little improvement. In reviewing the video of the lesson, Diane listened conceptually and realized that Deborah stopped each time her hands played together.

At the next lesson the teacher identified the problem of coordinating the hands in a steady rhythm. The girls tapped both hands counting out loud to solidify what beats the hands played together. Deborah played the right hand while both girls tapped the left hand. Then each took turns playing one hand of the piece so Deborah could hear both parts. Finally, Deborah played both hands with continuity. The teacher praised her success and reviewed the practice steps that improved Deborah's playing. Both girls had good practice in reading, rhythm, and coordination skills. As a result of Diane's conceptual planning, the coordination activities solved the problem of lack of continuity and improved the performance.

Teach to the Prepared Student. When one student comes prepared and the other student does not, how do you challenge both students? Whom do you teach, the faster or slower student? Of course you teach both, but design the lesson so the fastest will be challenged, while the slower will understand. In a children's group the teacher, Betty, taught Cori an assigned song that she had not practiced so she could catch up with Coltan, who had practiced. But Coltan had nothing to do, and it seemed unfair that Coltan received no instruction. Yes, it is unfair to penalize the prepared student, so it is advisable to teach to the prepared student. She could have assigned Coltan a song to learn independently while she helped Cori.

Students are motivated to practice for the group lesson. They feel a responsibility to the group to do their part. If we send a message that it is okay not to prepare, then group morale will suffer. At the same time, one can structure the lesson so both prepared and unprepared students will learn. Lessons organized around concepts will address both students' needs.

Plan Lessons Rich in Musical Concepts

Plan lessons that are rich in musical concepts, that appeal to students' expressiveness, and that enable the contrast of several approaches. Find a balance between introducing enough concepts to provide challenge while limiting the number of concepts to provide focus. For instance, if a student's scale playing is uneven, concepts to consider are tempo, rhythm, fingering, metric stress, dynamics, and technique. Any one of the related concepts may give direction to the student to improve the scale playing.

There is more than one solution to uneven scales, and each student in the group may use a different solution. Play in a slow tempo or in dotted rhythms with the metronome. Choose a legato fingering as it relates to the white and black keys. Play in a meter such as $\frac{4}{4}$ with a crescendo to beat one. Change the thumb placement on the key to eliminate unintended accents. Utilize many concepts in effective problem solving so that students benefit from learning more than one approach to playing a scale evenly.

Contrast Concepts. During the first year of study for a group of children, Diane used contrast of concepts effectively in a lesson on the touches of legato and staccato. First she told the students to play a piece legato, then she asked them to play the same piece staccato. They explored the similarities and differences between each student's legato and staccato performances. After they had experienced the touches, she asked them what symbols are used to show legato and staccato. This is an excellent demonstration of a direct experience in which students first explore the concept's sound and its physical production before defining the abstract symbol.

Jim also used contrast of touches in the first lesson with beginning college music majors. He explained and demonstrated five-finger scales and had the twelve students play several scales together. The sound was unmusical, with some students playing too loud. Jim gave a short lecture on posture and legato playing. An effective analogy was to compare playing the piano to playing on a teeter-totter. One end goes up when the other end goes down, just as one finger rises on the key as the next finger descends on the next key. Then he had the class play a scale together, and the legato sound was quite astonishing. The students looked amazed at having played a beautiful legato in a balanced ensemble sound.

Jim then directed them to play the scale staccato, which they found more difficult. The beauty of Jim's teaching is that he focused their attention on the sound and expressiveness of playing a scale, rather than only on the theoretical fact of the whole and half steps in a major scale.

Limit Concepts. In the first lesson with five beginning students ages eight to ten, Barbara ambitiously planned to teach note values of quarter, half, whole, and eighth notes; note reading from treble and bass clefs; and the dynamics of piano and forte. She introduced the symbols with flash cards and directed students to choose a piece in their method book, practice it, and play it for class.

The students had no idea how to relate the abstract symbols they saw on the flash cards to sounds on a piano. The class became one of individual lessons with the teacher trying to explain the symbols of each chosen piece. Other students waited impatiently for their turn with the teacher. The classroom became quite noisy with students running around the room. Barbara felt she had no control of the class and was very frustrated. In classes thereafter, she limited the number of concepts and provided activities to experience the concept, not just to name the symbol. She had students clap rhythms of each other's pieces and directed students to describe step and skip movement rather than pitch names. Limiting the concepts along with establishing rules of conduct helped the children focus their attention and enjoy their lesson.

Simplify. Refine the concept to its most basic level to help students understand the concept. Inexperienced teachers are often surprised when beginning students cannot identify the names of the notes on the piano or relate the grand staff to the piano. Many years have passed since their first lessons, so they don't remember those first experiences at the piano.

Notation in the most basic form can be described as symbols for sounds of high and low pitches. The high and low pitches are symbolized on the score by dots placed higher or lower on the page. The piano sounds, which are played horizontally, do not logically match the sound on a vertical page. Piano sounds are higher to the right and lower to the left, and the score symbols are up and down. Several clever teachers have solved this problem by turning the score sideways so the treble staff is to the right of the page matching the right side of the piano, and the bass staff is to the left of the page matching the left side of the piano. How inventive of these teachers to look at the staff differently, thus effectively simplifying the concept.

Unified Conceptual Lesson. Several concepts are explored in a lesson because each piece assigned may present different problems in the student's performance. However, keep in mind what concept was worked on in the previous piece and comment on it in the next piece. Contrasting similarities and differences within each activity is an excellent approach to group teaching. With the varied repertoire students can compare the concept in each of their pieces.

In another lesson with sisters Deborah and Angela, the teacher, Diane, kept a conceptual approach to many activities.

- She began with scales, hearing ones practiced, C and G major, and assigning new ones, D and A major. She asked what the scales had in common and students responded that the fingering and major scale pattern were the same.
- Then they played music with legato and staccato and discussed the different touches.
- She took them through a practice procedure to use with the newly assigned pieces. They walked the beat and clapped the rhythm while counting out loud. They identified similarities and differences in the music. They reviewed middle C position and C position, and sight read the new music in rhythm with continuity. They were urged to focus on intervals and up-and-down movement rather than note names. They identified similarities and differences between

songs in the assignment and discussed the moods that accompanying pictures conveyed.

Sight reading of new music provided a summary of the lesson, because the teacher reviewed all concepts explored—scale, touch, rhythm, intervals, and mood.

Teaching Unfamiliar Concepts. Don't avoid teaching concepts that are unfamiliar. A comprehensive curriculum will have theoretical concepts that teachers may not understand even though they can read the notes on the page. For instance, playing a composition in the Dorian mode is easy, but understanding why Dorian sounds different from major or minor may be difficult. Rather than avoid teaching an unfamiliar concept, study and learn about the new concept along with the students. Angela describes her learning experiences in teaching a college piano major class.

> I learned lots of new concepts when I was teaching the class. I didn't always know the concepts that I was going to teach, so sometimes I learned the new concepts just a few days before I taught them. I wasn't comfortable in teaching something that I just learned. However, I found that because I just learned it and I knew what problems the students should have, I could make my presentation more clear for them to understand.

Allowing oneself to be vulnerable and teach an unfamiliar concept can be advantageous, enabling teachers to identify with students' feelings when learning something new.

Limit Conditions

The problem design should limit the conditions of what is played so that the student can focus on the problem. For instance, limit the playing to a phrase instead of the whole piece. Assure the students you will only critique the concept in question. If you ask the students to name intervals in the melody as they play, do not require them to play the correct rhythm. Or the reverse—if you want to focus on the rhythm, accept wrong notes.

Make It Easy. Plan the students' playing so that they can be attentive to the problem. If you want them to hear and play a new chord progression, limit the conditions so they don't get tied up in matching notes and fingers rather than listening to the sound. Emily's objective in teaching modal improvisation to her college piano class was to define the primary chords of the Dorian, Phrygian, Lydian, and Mixolydian modes. The students were in their fifth month of piano study, and she planned the activities so that they could play easily and focus on the theoretical problem. She limited their playing to three primary chords in the mode. Without the coordination problem of playing both hands together, they could perform the chords well enough to hear the qualities created from progressions of i–II–VII in Phrygian, which emphasizes the lowered second degree of the scale, or I–II–v in Mixolydian, which emphasizes the lowered seventh.

They contrasted tension and release in I–IV–V in major and minor keys with modal primary triads, which is quite different.

Even if you have limited the conditions, anticipate that the playing may have to be further simplified for the student to be successful. If they cannot get it after a few tries, then simplify the playing. Barbara introduced ensemble playing to her college beginning class and anticipated that they would have trouble sight reading the notes and playing the rhythm at the same time. When they struggled with playing both hands, she directed them to play one hand and then distributed parts between the eight people so that all parts were heard in ensemble. The students played together successfully. These students were motivated by their success and eagerly worked on an assigned duet to practice and perform both hands together.

Students playing intermediate and advanced repertoire such as a Chopin Nocturne have so much to think about: pedal, phrase shape, rubato, ornaments, and balance of melody and accompaniment. If a student needs to focus on legato pedaling, for instance, another member of the group can play the melody while the student plays the left hand and pedals the chord changes. The student playing Chopin has a chance to hear all parts but focuses on pedaling and the other students are sight reading and learning new literature.

Classroom Management. Establish rules of behavior so that students can focus on the problem. When students are told what you expect in their behavior, then they can focus on the problem. With several pianos or keyboards in a room, the noise from several students playing different things at once can be chaotic. It is difficult for everyone to hear themselves and the teacher's instructions. Direct the students not to play out loud while the teacher is instructing and to mark the keys silently (play without depressing the keys or turn off the speaker on an electric piano). Marking allows the students to get a physical sensation of playing while hearing the teacher or student's demonstration.

Children expect rules of behavior and if not given, young students constantly test what they can and cannot do. Often the teacher becomes a disciplinarian in this situation, constantly criticizing the students for inappropriate behavior. Rather than set up such a negative, reactive climate, give students rules of behavior or better yet, have them decide the rules. They will more likely take responsibility for their behavior if they have participated in designing the rules. Class rules should be brief, simple to understand, and positive, such as respect each other and play only when directed to do so. Students are relieved and ready to learn when they know what is expected of them.

Musical Principles

The solutions chosen to solve a problem should be generalizations about the concept that can be transferred to a similar yet different situation. This is a most important step—the verification of the problem. Students will remember and use what they have learned if they understand what they have done. Some students can mimic the teacher or other students' playing and not realize that they have shaped a phrase or projected a melody beautifully. To check their understanding, have the students transfer the solution to another situation. To play a scale evenly, the student could transfer the solution of playing with appropriate accentuation in $\frac{4}{4}$ meter to another scale or to a scale passage in the student's repertoire. To clarify intervals of a melody, have the student transpose the melody to a different key using the same intervals. The student's success in transferring the concept will signal that he or she understands how to use the concept and will ensure that the idea will be used in practice.

In the group lesson generalizations through principles are especially important because several compositions will be heard at a lesson. If musical principles are compared between compositions played, then students will understand how topics talked about in each person's playing will affect their own playing. In a college piano class the objectives were playing five-finger minor scales and polishing individual solos for the midterm exam. The teacher, Eric, used scales to help the beginning students develop a relaxed facility in playing the piano. Eric noted problems when he observed that hands were tense and wrists were frozen as they played. Eric discussed hand balance and releasing the wrist to move in the direction of the finger being played (technique and pitch). They practiced the scales and also read a short piece applying the principle of hand balance. Next they played individual solos. However, Eric didn't transfer the hand balance principle to the solos, which would have extended their understanding. Application of the relaxed technique to a piece they knew well would have enabled them to feel and hear the difference in their playing.

Transfer Concepts. In order to encourage transfer of a concept between pieces, I asked Michelle, a graduate student-teacher, to use the following model for introducing tonic and dominant harmony to her beginning college music majors. The students' text introduces harmony with only the single-note, chord roots of the tonic and dominant rather than the full chord. The chord is difficult for beginning adults to coordinate and the roots focus their attention on the primary notes of the scale.

- Announce that the topic of the lesson will be harmonizing with tonic and dominant notes of the scale.
- As the students play five-finger major scales, direct them to name the first and fifth notes (tonic and dominant notes).
- Direct students to analyze and to write in I and V for tonic and dominant notes in their reading, transposing, and repertoire assignments.
- Improvise using only tonic and dominant notes and play rhythm exercises using the tonic note in the left hand and the dominant note in the right hand.

In the next lesson, Michelle taught sight reading and limited the pitch range to a fifth. Students were asked to identify the key of each of four examples and identify the tonic and dominant notes as they played. They were directed to write in the intervals and label I and V notes in both right and left hands. Next they transferred what they had learned about tonic and dominant by transposing what they had previously sight read. Then half of the class played a written melody and the other half chose either dominant or tonic notes to harmonize the melody. Next they improvised melodies in major five-finger scales while accompanying with the tonic or dominant notes, and were directed to end on the tonic. Focusing on the concept of tonic and dominant and comparing the similarities of tonic and dominant in several skills gave the lesson unity and direction and solidified the students' understanding.

Analogous Activities to Reinforce Concepts. Presenting a concept in activities away from the piano as well as playing the piano will help students make generalizations about the concept. Analogous activities such as walking, clapping, drawing, listening, and playing in the air engage students physically and mentally while exploring a concept. Betty introduced the half-note rhythm and *piano* and *forte* dynamics in her second lesson with seven-year-olds Cori and Coltan. She directed them to draw half notes for the right hand with stems up and for the left hand with stems down, and to write the counts for each half note. They prepared to play "I Hear the Echo" in the primer book of *Piano Adventures* by circling half notes, *p*, and *f*. They walked and clapped the half- and quarter-note rhythms of the piece and clapped loudly or softly for *forte* or *piano*. They studied two short rhythm patterns of quarter and half notes and chose which one their teacher played. They played "I Hear the Echo" and contrasted it with "Wind in the Trees," which has the same concepts. The varied activities helped Cori and Coltan hear the differences between quarter and half notes and *piano* and *forte* and realize the similarities of the concepts through playing several pieces and listening and writing rhythm patterns.

Functional Skills

Understanding a general principle is best verified by transferring the principle to another skill. Often called functional skills, reading, transposing, improvising, harmonizing, playing by ear, and mirroring require students to think about many concepts. Fun activities for the children's groups in the preparatory program at Wichita State University are improvising, playing melodies by ear, and transposing melodies to all major and minor five-finger scales. After two months of study in the *Keyboard Explorer* by Guy Duckworth, they have a good background for applying principles of rhythm and pitch to the staff, and they begin playing Christmas carols with ease. Because of their aural training, they hear melodic intervals and rhythmic patterns. They readily apply what they already know about pitch and rhythm from playing by ear to reading because they can relate the position on the staff to their "inner ear" of how the music should sound. This is very different from playing by rote in which students imitate rather than understand. Because students had to figure out the intervals of step, skip, and repeat from their singing, they had an analytical basis for understanding pitch and could readily apply it to reading.

Diane, a graduate student-teacher, often introduced theoretical concepts by asking probing questions that encouraged students to think about the concept. She asked her multi-level college piano class, "How and why are triad inversions used in music?" This was an appropriate question to ask the students, who were in four different levels of the proficiency curriculum, because each was required to play a chord progression of varied difficulty. Students studied the history of figured bass and substituted popular chord symbols for figured bass. Diane directed them to harmonize a melody and asked why the chords are inverted rather than always in root position. The students began to hear and feel in their hands the difference between accompanying with the disjunct sound and physically awkward movement of root position chords, as opposed to the smooth sound and physically pianistic movement created by chord inversions. They experimented with inversions for good voice leading in harmonizing a melody and in their required chord progression.

College students want to understand the reason behind what they are playing. Thus, the principle was defined: smooth voice leading between chords is created by chord inversions (harmony, legato articulation, pitch movement). Each line of a four-voice chord progression moves mostly by step and small skips when inversions are used. Each line moves by large leaps when root positions are used. The principle can be applied to their understanding of all music. They can apply voice leading to music they harmonize, memorize, and improvise, as well as music they play in orchestra and band or sing in opera and choir.

This is an excellent example of the rhythm of learning from ambiguous goals to clear ones (Chapter 3). Rather than lecturing students about triad inversions, Diane asked an open-ended question to involve the students in thinking about the issue. Then as students gathered information and experienced playing inversions, they discovered the principle of voicing. The progression from vagueness to clarity must not be interrupted for student insight to occur.

Transpose. Transpose what is read to clarify key and interval relationships. Often students play with better accuracy in transposing because they are forced to read by relationships—scale degrees and intervals within the scale. Too often they read note to note by letter name instead of seeing intervals and chord patterns within a key. The ability to transpose serves a pianist well by accommodating voice ranges, by understanding transposing instruments, and by adding variety to accompaniments for hymn singing. In addition, transposing is a most valuable resource in learning to read music. Paul, a seven-year-old beginning student, played several melodies by ear and transposed them to major and minor five-finger patterns during the first two months of study. Because he had learned interval and key relationships, he bypassed the primer method book and seemed comfortable playing not only the initial pieces in the level one method book but pieces in the middle and end of the book as well. His accelerated progress was in large part due to his ability to transpose at ease in all keys.

Improvise. Improvising is an excellent test of all concepts learned. When students make up a melody on a given rhythm pattern using 2nds with some leaps of 3rds, 4ths, and 5ths, they demonstrate their understanding of melodic intervals and rhythm. By improvising two four-measure phrases, students show they understand the formal unit of a phrase and choose pitches, rhythms, and chords that contribute to phrase tension and release. Stylistic improvisations based on classic, romantic, and jazz idioms demonstrate a complex understanding of music. The ability to improvise accompaniments to a lead line or hymn tune is not only gratifying but helps students recognize chord structures in written music.

Play by Ear. Playing by ear is a skill that requires students to evaluate key, meter, melodic intervals, phrase lengths, and chord progressions. Many piano students have not developed aural awareness. They can play notes on the piano without having to really hear pitch direction. Helping students sing accurately will greatly improve their sensitivity to pitch in playing the piano. Train students to discriminate between higher and lower sounds, steps and leaps, and half and whole steps. Their voices may not respond at first to what they hear, but with consistent practice and coaching in raising or lowering their voices, students will begin matching pitches.

Playing melodies they know by ear is an excellent motivation for ear training. Nearly all pianists have been asked to play "Happy Birthday" at gatherings of family and friends. How embarrassing not to be able to play it, especially if many years of piano have trained one to play more difficult literature than this simple song. In order to play "Happy Birthday," students listen and analyze the features of the song.

1) Melody (leaps of thirds, fourths, fifths, sixths, and an octave)
2) Meter ($\frac{3}{4}$)
3) Key (usually F major)
4) Upbeats (starts on beat 3)
5) Harmony (I–IV–V7 with a V7–I cadence at the end)
6) Non-harmonic tones (often dissonant neighbor tones on beat 1)
7) Harmonic rhythm (chords in dotted half notes on beat 1)

Therefore, to play by ear requires analyzing many concepts, which are similar concepts in the students' repertoire. Playing by ear is an excellent reinforcement for reading music because it develops good habits of thinking about multiple concepts.

Not only do these functional skills have immediate use in themselves, they require us to analyze and think about the construction of the music. A habit of analysis of music played will lead to a deeper understanding of the score and thus a more sensitive performance.

Mirror. A very useful skill that is not often used is that of mirroring pitches between hands. The benefits of the skill are better eye-hand coordination, effortless technique, and quick perception of interval relationships. It's rather amazing that a skill with such far-reaching effects would be so neglected. As with other functional skills the initial learning curve is difficult, but with repeated practice, mirroring can become second nature.

Play a chromatic scale in contrary motion beginning on D or A flat, and note the mirror image of the black or white keys of the other hand. In the D chromatic scale, therefore, C sharp in the left hand mirrors E flat in the right hand.

Then C mirrors E, B mirrors F, and so on throughout the octave. Only the D and A flat chromatic scales naturally mirror the other hand. One can mirror any passage of music with this information, but expect the sound to be dissonant. Consider the mirror of the first notes of Beethoven's "Für Elise." E, D sharp would be mirrored by C, C sharp. Keep the same fingering in both hands so that if the fifth finger in the right hand plays, the fifth finger in the left hand plays, then the fourth. This balance of the hands is amazingly comfortable, because of the use of the same topography and the same fingers.

Beginning students will mirror more easily than advanced students, because they are not accustomed to parallel motion within a key signature. Many well-known teachers throughout pedagogical history have used mirroring in their teaching (Duckworth, *Keyboard Musician;* Fink; Ganz).

Motivation

Problem solving is only effective if the student is interested in working on a problem. The teacher may select problem spots in the playing, but if the student is not cooperative, the playing does not improve. A good way to determine students' needs and interest is to ask them. Before they play ask them what they need to focus on in the lesson. Also after they play, ask them to critique the playing. In both instances address their area of interest. The teacher may be concerned that necessary corrections won't be made, but most of the time the teacher's concerns are satisfied even though the focus is on the student's needs. Students do ask the right questions if we give them a chance.

Emily, a teaching assistant, wrote about intrinsic goals in a beginning college piano class.

> I think the piano class should be the place where they discover their interest in piano playing and learn for themselves, not only for the piano proficiency exam. If they can learn for their own purposes, they will learn more in the four semesters required or they will soon forget everything they learned after the piano proficiency exam and maybe never play the piano again.

Is piano class for the college music major just another requirement for the degree? Beyond this extrinsic goal, how can students be motivated to practice and progress in piano study, so they are more intrinsically motivated? Music majors choose the degree because they have some proficiency on an instrument or voice and come to the piano class with little or no background in playing the piano. They often are uncomfortable with the instrument because of having to play two hands with several notes at a time. A common concern is "I can't read bass clef and play hands together." Although areas of problem solving discussed earlier help address students' concerns, most basic is their perceived need to learn the concept being discussed. Rather than presenting a chord progression to be played in all keys as an end in itself, help students understand why they are learning it and why they move their fingers in a certain way. Sing the progression in four-part harmony and compare the direction and intervals of each voice to music they sing in choir or parts they play in band. They learn that music is written with voices moving smoothly a second or third apart rather than jumping a fourth or fifth apart. Thus they see the need for inverting chords from their root positions for smooth voice leading.

Before presenting abstract theoretical information, let students know the assignment for using the information. If they know their responsibilities, they will be more motivated to listen to the lecture. Diane presented a lesson on several types of seventh chords and identified the notes of the chords and styles of music using particular seventh chords. It was suggested that she preface her lecture by giving the students their assignment using seventh chords, so that they could be thinking about how to apply the information to their assignment. The four students in the group study different levels of the college curriculum according to their previous background. The level two student's assignment was to play all types of seventh chords on every pitch, the level three student's assignment was to improvise a melody and accompany with given seventh chords in close inversions, and the level four student's assignment was to prepare an arrangement from a lead line (melody with chord symbols given). When students know what is expected of them, they will be much more actively involved in the lecture and discussion because they want to understand how to complete their assignment.

Megan, my student who is a sophomore in high school, was asked to accompany a singer for the school talent show. After hearing Megan and her vocalist read the score, the director asked her to change what was written so the vocalist could have more flexibility and the piano part would be more interesting. Megan had been learning to improvise in her piano lessons by playing sing-and-strum accompaniments (no melody line), using fill-ins, and reading popular chord symbols. She was excited to try and apply what she had learned to a real performance. In the next lesson she wanted to know what to do to give the vocalist more flexibility and to not cover up the melody. She was reminded of the sing-and-strum style that leaves out the melody. She arranged the chords so that she had a richer sound with an octave bass in the left hand and chords in the right hand. She was careful to keep the right-hand chords outside the melodic range so the singer could be heard. She added rhythm patterns to project the style and arpeggios at phrase endings to propel the music forward to the next vocal entrance. The lesson was invigorating with this very motivated student.

Students have to want to learn in order to learn. If we respect their goals and ask them about their musical concerns, students will participate more actively in the lesson. Let them know the reasons behind what is being taught so that they can understand the purpose of the topic for the lesson. Help students relate what they are learning in piano to other areas of their musical life—music theory and history, instrumental and vocal performance—so they understand they are learning music, not just piano.

Group Activities for Learning Concepts

Students often learn more when they are not put on the spot to perform. They can listen to a peer play and test their assessment against the teacher's and other students' evaluations. In order for each student to be involved in one another's musical problems, the teacher must engage each student musically and intellectually. Following are suggestions for teaching musical concepts in groups.

Performance. Students in groups will play the same music part of the time and play individually assigned repertoire most of the time. In an individual lesson, the teacher listens to pieces assigned and makes corrections. In a group setting, the listening student will be included in the learning process of the playing student. Ask the students to listen for accuracy of notes and rhythms and evidence of style and phrasing. After the playing, let the listening students give their comments, always beginning with a positive comment of what was played well and following with suggestions for improvement. When students are aware they must listen and evaluate the performance, they often will identify the problems that the teacher wants to pursue.

Rhythm. To work on rhythm inaccuracies in the performance, have all students tap or clap the rhythm while counting out loud, then continue clapping and counting while the performer plays. The closer the students sit together, the more likely the performer will be influenced. Students can share the same bench or stand directly beside the performer. A student could also point to notes while the performer plays. Classmates could sight read two or four measures of the performing student's repertoire while he listens, claps, and evaluates the difference in his performance of the rhythms.

What is the least favorite instruction to a student? You guessed it, "Count out loud!" It is difficult to coordinate two hands, find correct pitches, pedal, and at the same time count out loud. It is hard to say the right counts in pulse while playing. Participating in a group that is always counting out loud together sets up a positive attitude about counting. Rhythm counted together is habit-forming and takes the pressure off the individual to say the counts correctly. With beginning students, associate rhythm with pulse when clapping or tapping rhythms. Students must learn to separate the two concepts of rhythm and pulse. Rhythm is the changing note values of half, quarter, and eighth. Pulse is the ever-constant, unchanging beat. To avoid confusion for a beginning student, associate rhythm with clapping, and pulse with walking. While seated at the piano, step the beat, sway the upper body, and clap the rhythm while saying the words or beats. In introducing a new piece, simplify the movement by walking and swaying to the beat while chanting the words, then add clapping, then add counting.

Meter. Older students can coordinate conducting the beat while stepping the rhythms. Involving the whole body internalizes rhythm with the beat, so it is felt rather than intellectualized. Conducting gives the advanced student sophisticated information about relative stress in a measure and in a phrase, and stepping the rhythms helps the student associate rhythm impetus with the metric structure.

Technique. Teachers should insist that students watch one another in order to learn from one another. For instance, in teaching technique in a group have the students observe each other to assess rounded hand shapes, firm fingers, and relaxed wrists. Seeing each other's different hand shapes will help students evaluate if they are playing correctly.

Reading. Reading music is a skill of associating symbols with sound. Analogous activities away from the piano help students understand pitch as sounds that move up, down, and stay the same. Help students develop good habits of learning each new piece through study of the piece away from the piano.

- Draw in the air the shape of the melody.
- Shape the specific up-down-same movements.
- Sing the step-skip-repeat movement of the melody.

Beginning melodies are within a five-note range so hand shapes from the waist to the top of the head could represent each pitch. Students can watch each other to see if they match their classmate's shapes. Next, transfer directional and intervallic reading to the piano.

- Direct one student to play while others say the up-down-same and step-skip-repeat movement of the melody.
- Repeat with each student.

Students will associate music reading with sound instead of reading individual note names on a staff. In fact only the beginning note of a pattern needs to be named in directional reading. Too often we drill note names, which does not help them play with continuity. It takes too long to associate an A on the staff with an A on the piano. However, if they figure out the first note, all they have to do is read up and down by step or skip for an accurate reading of the score.

Style. Style and interpretation can be taught in an intermediate and advanced group. Ask students to listen to each other's performance of music from different style periods and imitate the style in their own playing. For instance, a student who plays with too much rubato in a Brahms Intermezzo could imitate the style of another student playing a Bach Prelude. Or a student who plays Bach too dryly for the piano could play like the student playing Brahms and interpret with more nuance. Students could then evaluate the result and give feedback to the performer. Often the performance is much improved.

Suggested Reading

Duckworth, *Keyboard Explorer.*
——, *Keyboard Musician*, Book VI: *The Symmetrical Keyboard.*

Fink, *Mastering Piano Technique.*
Ganz, *Exercises for Piano: Contemporary and Special.*

Further Thought

Give a synopsis of the main considerations in planning group lessons that encourage independent problem solving. In a class situation divide into small groups with each group taking one or two points to discuss.

1. Challenge
2. Concepts
3. Limit conditions
4. Principles and transfer
5. Functional skills
6. Motivation

12 Group Dynamics

Teaching in groups has become commonplace today. Some instructors teach lessons to children and adults in groups on a weekly basis. Others group students into master classes to perform for one another, ensembles to play duets, and music theory groups to learn fundamentals. Teachers expect students to do their best in these settings, but sometimes they do not. Children may be inattentive, disruptive, or may fail to work together on the lesson. College students may be unresponsive to questions, may play mechanically, and may fail to concentrate. They might respond very well in an individual lesson, which leads the instructor to wonder why they are not doing their best in the group lesson.

Students in productive groups concentrate on the lesson, play musically, discuss their playing with the teacher and other students, and excel in their playing and understanding. Why is the lesson going so well with students playing better than either the teacher or they imagined they could?

Groups are conducive to nurturing students to play with understanding and skill. Each individual is unique and bringing students together to learn music can enhance their success. Positive synergy exists between students in a productive group. Following are characteristics of productive groups and their opposites.

- Active involvement, not passive
- Cooperative, not competitive
- Highest level of excellence, not the lowest common denominator
- Individual differences, not conformity
- Open-minded and flexible, not stubborn
- Spontaneous, expressive, thoughtful performances; not inhibited, colorless performances
- Attitude that each individual is responsible to do his best, not to slide by because others will do it
- Care and respect for each other, not prejudice and cliques
- Challenge, not boredom
- Insight, not regurgitating facts
- Enthusiasm, not dread
- Trust, not fear

Therefore, the type of groups described here are those in which students are high-achieving, ones that extend their individual thinking so that they perform at a higher level of productivity. As teachers, how do we foster such lofty characteristics? In a group setting the teacher becomes a facilitator. No longer are lecturing and modeling the primary modes of communication. Instead, the teacher encourages discussion and student demonstrations. No longer will the teacher's goals be the primary ones. Instead, the teacher facilitates the planning of students' goals. No longer will one interpretation be the correct one. Instead, the teacher enlarges the musical context to allow many viable interpretations.

For help in facilitating groups, the discipline of social psychology is of great assistance to piano teachers. According to Dorwin Cartwright and Alvin Zander, "desirable consequences from groups can be deliberately enhanced" (23). How can the teacher assist students through the group-growth stages to help create a healthy group? A teacher's attitude is one of openness, flexibility, caring, and a desire for students to take responsibility for their own learning. In order to guide students through the group-growth stages, teachers must be willing to sacrifice their authority and allow students to discover musical concepts. If we constantly tell students what to do and how to play, then we fail to give them a chance to be themselves. We only see what we want to see, not who the students really are. Instead, take pleasure in getting to know their likes, dislikes, strengths, weaknesses, musical interests, and personalities. Conversations between students and the teacher allow students to learn about each other and about music.

A conversational tone in the group lesson enables the positive dynamics within a group to flourish. Students work cooperatively to improve their understanding and playing. Individuals practice and come prepared to learn because of a strong sense of responsibility to do their part. They look forward to lessons knowing that they will have a chance to warm up, try out ideas, and demonstrate what they know. They are willing to take risks to change their playing, and they consider their failures a part of learning.

Principles derived from inquiry into group dynamics can assist teachers in facilitating groups. Following are principles to consider in teaching piano in groups (Table 12.1). Each principle will be discussed and examples given from actual lessons. The first principle, that the group aids in problem solving, was the topic of Chapter 11.

The Group Leadership Is Most Efficient
When It Is Participatory

Teachers want to help students become independent thinkers so they can continue to enjoy music and solve problems in their practice. Too often we tell students what to correct in their practice and have them imitate our playing. Asking questions and building on ideas that students suggest will make them think. Students can express themselves and test their understanding through peer reaction. Students tend to be more curious about the subject matter and initiate questions and comments about the music when the teacher balances indirect and direct comments (Chapter 7). Often in this climate of musical interchange, the teacher is enriched as well by learning from the students.

As a facilitator the teacher has to let go of control. She has to trust that students can think independently, evaluate problems in performances, and give

Table 12.1

Group Dynamics Principles

1. The group aids in problem solving.

2. The group leadership is most efficient when it is participatory.

3. Group participation lessens inhibitions, whereas individual playing develops self-esteem.

4. The group depends on each individual to do her part.

5. The group functions most efficiently with a spirit of cooperation.

6. The group is a medium of change.

good suggestions to improve performance. Expect students to give ideas and prod them to do so. When the attitude of active participation is established in the lesson, students begin taking leadership responsibilities. The lesson becomes one of shared leadership with the teacher assuming leadership when necessary— being willing to share but not dominate leadership responsibilities.

Diane, a student-teacher, ably facilitated a master class by asking students to evaluate each other's playing. She let go of an ego need to tell them what she thought and ingeniously pursued their evaluations. She told me after the lesson that she listened to their playing, evaluated musical problems, and made herself delay her thoughts until she heard student comments. Her most effective teaching strategy was to ask students for their evaluations of the playing before she gave her evaluation. Students had to think about the playing and answer verbally. They astutely observed strengths of technique and interpretation in each other's playing as well as weaknesses of dynamics and phrase shaping. Diane built on their ideas to help them find solutions to performance problems. Rather than telling students what they already know, the instructor should allow them to cite the problem so that they are immediately involved and ready to solve the problem.

A healthy pattern of communication is of utmost importance to the group process. Group lessons fail if teachers tell students what to do, criticize their playing, and require them to play by imitation. Students are much more likely to be dependent, compliant, or counter-dependent when teachers use only direct communication of giving directions, criticizing, and lecturing. When teachers balance indirect communication—asking questions and accepting and building on student's ideas—with directions and critiques, however, students tend to think for themselves, contribute to discussion, and trust their intuitions.

Group Participation Lessens Inhibitions, Whereas Individual Playing Develops Self-Esteem

For students to progress and be motivated to practice, their basic psychological needs of self-esteem and feelings of success must be met. So many factors affect a student's sense of self-esteem. Students come to a lesson with experiences from home, school, and with classmates. Their disposition toward confidence or insecurity is shaped by their backgrounds. Piano teachers can influence students' confidence by preparing them for success musically and by giving positive constructive feedback.

Teachers want students to play well, progress consistently, and feel good about playing the piano. No one wants to merely correct mistakes in lessons. Instead, teachers can anticipate what problems students might have and guide their thinking so they are prepared to play well.

When students come to a lesson, they may be thinking about what has happened at school or with friends rather than about playing the piano. Starting a lesson is much like an exercise warm-up period before the hard work can begin. We try to focus students' attention on the piano lesson and on their problems and successes in practice. A group lesson is an ideal setting to warm up students for the piano lesson. Students can talk about their day with one another for a few minutes, or the teacher can lead a discussion on practice and problems in the repertoire. A few minutes of sharing can get students involved in the lesson mentally and physically. Also, playing together rather than individually allows students time to start thinking about piano.

If we begin the lesson by checking on each item of the assignment—scales, review pieces, and new pieces—students may make mindless mistakes because they may not feel at ease. When mistakes happen, this is a clue to change directions in the lesson. Rather than putting the student in the spotlight, do things together such as playing scales to help them feel comfortable so they can do their best at the lesson.

Teachers sometimes err by having students only play together in the college piano class with multiple keyboards. Students get frustrated when they cannot hear themselves and tend to play too loud. One solution is to play together to try out the idea, then individually to hear their playing. A graduate teaching assistant directed a class of twelve college students to improvise using a five-finger major scale. Even though the key, meter, and digital accompaniment unified the playing, the sound was loud, dissonant, and ugly. Improvising together gave them a chance to try out the concept without fear of mistakes. Next, they improvised one at a time with enjoyment, and were ready to perform and demonstrate their creativity and musicality. Playing individually allowed class members to hear one another's ideas. Students gained confidence as they heard their classmates play and decided they could do it, too.

Another error in class piano teaching is the constant use of headphones for instruction because it isolates students from one another and squelches the many possibilities of learning together. A balance can be struck between practicing alone and playing for others. Eric used the headphones effectively when he reviewed an assignment in which the students named chord tones in primary triads. He directed students in harmonizing a melody with figured bass symbols. As he talked through a microphone and played at the teacher's digital piano, students listened through headphones and followed his directions at their pianos. In this way students clarified their understanding before playing the assignment for the teacher. Later Eric had the students give their neighbor a chord symbol and key to name the notes. After answering, the student gave a chord symbol to the next student. Eric prepared them to be successful; therefore, students became confident with figured bass and were motivated to find the chord tones. Students were pleased with correct answers, yet mistakes were okay and viewed as a source of learning.

The principle of lessening inner restraints was vivid in my mind in the second lesson with a freshman piano major class. Students were very tentative and quiet during the first class. Students take this class to learn the skills of sight reading, transposing, harmonizing, improvising, and playing by ear. These are skills that piano majors have almost never attempted and they feel very inhibited about showing their ignorance. They are accustomed to memorizing and polishing repertoire. They are "safe" with previously learned repertoire, but functional skills often make many students very vulnerable and fearful of mistakes.

To lessen the students' inhibitions, my plan for the second class was to interact by playing duets, transposing, and harmonizing together. They were directed to help each other until the duet and functional skills were perfected. The digital piano laboratory with a lesson controller and headphones enabled grouping of two to four students. The duos worked on chord inversions and chord progressions and presented their solutions of fingering and chord spellings to the class on the visualizer (a display that lights notes played on the digital piano). They listened and graded each other's transposition and harmonization assignments. Then they sight read Clementi Sonatinas in a two-piano version with the original and an accompaniment.

During this interaction I served as a facilitator by directing the activities. I observed the students relaxing, probably because they noticed that their neighbor made mistakes, too, which is acceptable in this class. They realized they had similar questions about music theory. In this atmosphere of learning, encouragement, asking questions, and experiencing some success with a new skill, the students relaxed and began to try their best without constant fear of humiliation. They became immersed in the concepts and skills being learned rather than submitting to their negative inner voices saying, "I can't do it."

An effective group lesson balances activities that lessen students' inhibitions with those that spotlight their individual achievements. Students need times where they can think and experiment without fear of ridicule for making mistakes. If teachers trust that students are capable, they will delay criticism until students have had a chance to warm up. Students' opinions must be heard in order for them to gain confidence in their abilities. Because of the diversity of individuals, each student will have ideas that other students can learn from. When disagreements occur between students, they learn from each other. Students are challenged to reevaluate their way of thinking and often conceive an idea together that no one person could have thought of by themselves. The group lesson enables students to develop confidence in themselves and their piano playing.

The Group Depends on Each Individual to Do His or Her Part

Positive group morale is dependent on students attending lessons regularly and being prepared. When members are either absent from lessons or have not practiced, the group morale suffers. The errant student has let down the group members and teacher. They have shirked their responsibility to be prepared and actively participate in the group. The students who are present feel a loss and may not perform their best.

At the interview or first class, give students and parents a clear statement of attendance policies and practice requirements. Let them know what is expected of them and hold them to it. Ensure a long-term commitment to the group lessons by charging tuition by the term or semester. Give careful thought to scheduling so that the students' varied schedules will align and they will be assured that the group lesson is a priority. If group lessons are once a month rather than weekly, inquire about students' schedules and change the time and day to accommodate all students. The hassle will be worth it when all attend. Organize groups for second-year and intermediate levels as well as beginning levels. Meeting with their peers is a great motivation to attend lessons regularly.

For monthly performance classes, select a piece that the student plays well and assign it to be heard in the performance class. Students invest time in polishing music that they know they will be performing. If students wait to choose a piece the day of the class, the performance will probably suffer.

In the college piano class a semester consists of about sixteen weeks of lessons. The course syllabus should list practice requirements, attendance policy, test dates, and weekly assignments based on the curriculum to be studied. Give dates for midterm tests and finals. Continue to communicate these requirements verbally throughout the semester and contact students if they are failing or have excessive absences. Juggling course responsibilities with their social lives may overwhelm college students, especially those living away from home for the first time. Contacting them promptly may be enough to convince them to attend to their course study and practice.

College students attend class when they are motivated to learn and when the teacher and classmates expect them to be there. Students will be motivated to prepare the assignment if they know it will be heard weekly. The expectation of preparation develops when students regularly play the assignment for a peer, the class, or the teacher. Therefore, students feel a responsibility to attend and be prepared. This intrinsic motivation is much more effective than extrinsic motivation that penalizes students for absences by lowering grades.

The difference in intrinsic and extrinsic motivation was exemplified in a class of twelve freshmen music majors. They were practicing, attending class, and enjoying good group morale until midterm. Tests at midterm are stressful and the less-prepared and less-confident students began to miss class. When the attendance policy was stressed again—three consecutive absences or five overall lower the letter grade one letter—other students began missing class. In fact, a majority of the members had four absences but not more than two consecutive, as if they were planning their days off. Group morale suffered because students were not there to participate, and the energy level dropped. When absent students came back unprepared, presentations had to be repeated. A month went by and finally the teacher placed less stress on the attendance policy and more on the music to be prepared for the final. Students got back into the swing of being responsible in attendance and practice. Once again group morale was positive. Intrinsic motivation of wanting to play well encouraged students to attend regularly.

It is human nature to react defensively when a student is absent. The teacher asks, How could they miss my class? The lessons are prepared to be interesting, musical, and enjoyable. What message is the student sending? So many events affect the college students' lives: the used car won't start, they slept through the alarm, they woke up sick, or they decided not to come to class because they hadn't practiced sufficiently. The class syllabus should stress that students should call before the missed class to excuse an absence. Then the teacher will know the reason and also be able to tell the other students. A student's absences indicate to the teacher that a problem exists and a conference may be necessary to understand the student's situation. Be attentive to non-verbal body language and behavior. If they are vague about a problem, ask further questions and accept their feelings if they have difficulty expressing themselves.

The Group Functions Most Efficiently with a Spirit of Cooperation

Less productivity in a group may be a result of competition among group members, according to group dynamics researchers. Students in groups who cooperate were found to be more effective in reaching the goal. Students in the cooperative group value each other's ideas, offer more diverse ideas, work together to achieve the goal, and are friendlier to one another. Students who are competitive may be less secure personally and may have expectations of hostility from others (Deutsch 482). The teacher can influence the degree of cooperation or competition in a group. The goal of the lesson activity, the evaluation of the product, and the style of interaction all influence students' attitudes.

The teacher may unknowingly encourage competition by asking, "Were any mistakes made?" Students will find fault with each other, if they only notice mistakes. To encourage cooperation in a group, ask the students what was played well. If the teacher begins with the positive and shows appreciation for the students' efforts, then group members will follow her model. Positive remarks after each performance do not signify approval for a poor or mediocre performance but a response to the person for the effort. The courtesy of responding is vital to encouraging a cooperative working relationship.

Beginning with positive comments prepares the students for constructive criticism. After positive comments are made, ask students to suggest what will improve the playing. As trust develops between group members, they will be able to give ideas freely without hurting each other's feelings. The student will know that classmates are trying to respond in the performer's best interests. They are working hard toward the goal of improving the performance.

Six-year-olds CeCe, James, and Jasmine learn to work cooperatively under Eric's guidance. His goal in the lesson is to develop a steady beat. Students each take a turn accompanying with a steady beat on the wood block, while the others dance and sway to the music from a CD. The students are cooperative because they know they will get their chance to play the wood block. Students are very aware if the group setting is fair to them. As they develop attitudes about membership in the group, they expect a setting that will value each of them and give each a chance to do their best work. If the cooperative setting does not develop, they spend their energy competing for "status" in the group.

In another lesson the children misbehaved during a eurhythmics activity. Eric had them pass a ball to one another in a steady beat to his improvised music. He changed the tempo from slower to faster and they had difficulty coordinating the faster movements. They became frustrated and James left the group with the ball, while CeCe started exaggerating her motions inappropriately. Eric reprimanded James and told him to sit down and do what he was supposed to, and he scolded CeCe for her inappropriate movements. Eric's criticism of their behavior led to hostile feelings between group members during the activity, each blaming the other for getting into trouble. He used "no" and "don't" several times in this episode. What could Eric have done to anticipate problems that might frustrate this age group? Removing the object, the ball in this case, which was causing the disruption may have defused the situation, rather than using negative words to change students' behavior. Additionally, simplifying the activity will keep students involved. Because the smaller movements of passing the ball at a faster tempo frustrated them, move students closer together and clap or tap the beat with smaller motions. The less children hear "no," and the more the teacher praises good behavior, the more positive the environment will be.

A group of two young students, Kristine and Dana, were taking group lessons with Mike, a graduate student in piano pedagogy. Kristine and Dana were treating each other poorly. While one was playing the other would play louder (not the same song). The teacher's attempts at restoring order were ignored. The students were competing for the teacher's attention. If the students misbehave, trust that they want to learn to play the piano and find ways to make them successful. As Mike's supervisor, he asked me to teach the group for him to observe. My goal was to encourage the girls to work together, value their own accomplishments, and value each other's efforts. To encourage cooperation I directed them to listen to one another and evaluate the accuracy of the dotted quarter rhythm in each other's playing. If they heard inaccurate counting, they were expected to respond and work together to solve the problem. They were quiet at first, but with questions and encouragement they responded positively to one another and appreciated each other's efforts.

Angela, a graduate student-teacher, describes how her students learned from one another, even when views conflicted.

> The students shared their experience with their particular Bartók *Mikrokosmos* piece they had prepared for the midterm. Everyone learned some valuable information and from many different points of view. I felt this was a much more interesting way to learn about Bartók's pieces than coming from one source—the teacher. Not everyone agreed about his or her feelings of contemporary music. Not everyone saw Bartók in the same light. Despite these differences they seemed to appreciate each others' viewpoints and came away learning more than they would have by themselves.

A difficult problem in teaching groups is what to do when one student progresses faster than another. If we help the student who does not understand, we feel like we are wasting the time of the faster student. This situation could become a competitive one with the faster student "acting out" in competing for the teacher's attention. Angela describes her experience with a group of kindergarten through third-grade students.

> I do not feel as comfortable with a large group of children. They are more demanding of my attention and much more dependent than my college class. I feel I am constantly answering someone's questions or attending to a student while neglecting the group as a whole. Perhaps teaching a smaller group, three or four children, would have been more valuable to me as a learning experience. Another frustrating problem is that the students are at different levels. Perhaps if the coordinator of the program had interviewed them, we could have found a more compatible group. I have also learned to listen beyond the words. I have learned that Frederick's "I'm bored" actually means "I need attention."

The teacher's frustration with this group of eight students is common to teachers who are new to a group setting. Her solutions are insightful as well. Piano groups need homogeneity by age and ability in order to develop cooperation and productivity. Such grouping is conducive for students to be equally involved in a problem. In this group, students' ages ranged from five to eight, some with no background, others with some musical training. Frederick had previous musical training and quickly understood each concept presented. While Angela was helping the other students, Frederick said he was bored and did things to demand her attention, such as sitting in her lap. Of course this was distracting and annoying to the teacher and students. The lesson deteriorated into students competing for the teacher's attention rather than learning music. Later lessons were planned thoroughly, anticipating the children's behavior in the various activities. She asked Frederick to explain a concept and lead a rhythmic activity. She allowed other students leadership opportunities as well. Angela describes her success with a rhythmic activity that encouraged cooperation: "In the children's group they imitated each other's clapped rhythms. They loved the activity and it encouraged a spirit of cooperation in which they were able to learn more easily."

Some advice to follow in the above situation is to teach to the fastest student. Plan the lesson so that all students are challenged. Allow students to help in planning the lesson. Assigning more difficult music may challenge the fast student. While students are playing together, ask the more advanced student to observe the dynamics and shape the phrase. Since music concepts are the same for all levels of difficulty, students can listen to the more advanced student play more difficult music and hear, for instance, if the pulse is steady or if dynamics are observed. If competition persists despite the teacher's efforts, regroup the students so peers on a similar level will challenge the advanced student. Constantly question if the students are in a setting that provides optimum opportunities for learning. Adjust the teaching style, materials, and grouping so learning is maximized.

Students are more engaged in thinking and improve their performance when the teacher designs a cooperative environment. Students' energies are directed toward improving their understanding and playing in a cooperative setting, and they don't have to expend energy defending themselves or acting disruptive to cover up their feelings and insecurities.

The Group Is a Medium of Change

Students in groups influence each other's attitudes about learning and can change one another's way of thinking about the topic. Groups work most effectively when learning from one another is encouraged. Teachers choreograph a lesson so that students see and hear one another play. They facilitate interaction between the students so that they form opinions and hear other opinions about music. Teachers can structure the group lesson to build morale and positive attitudes about each other and playing the piano.

The least effective approach in a piano class is to teach each student individually while other students are practicing using headphones. A group lesson is not a collection of two to twelve individual lessons in the same room. Each student must be equally involved with the topic and with each other in learning about the topic. So many opportunities for learning are lost when students are isolated. A lesson that is going badly could deteriorate further if the teacher directs students to put on headsets to work individually. This is usually a frustrating situation for teacher and students.

The teacher can facilitate supportive groups by encouraging students to interact and learn from one another. Instead of the teacher answering questions, have the other students answer. Divide the class into small groups of 2–4 (subgroup), give them a problem to solve, let them work together, and have them present their solutions to the whole class. Small groups can observe each other's hand position, posture, and pedaling. Students can be subgrouped into two or more in a piano laboratory by using the headphone communication system. Students can play assignments for each other, clap rhythms, practice duets, and critique fingering and notes in scale playing.

Subgrouping Classes. Larger groups of more than four people require subgrouping into smaller units so that each student can participate fully. In a larger group a few people will do most of the talking and playing. Subgrouping a class of twelve into groups of four gives every student a chance to play and give ideas. A digital piano laboratory with headsets provides flexible grouping. After subgroups have prepared the assignment, students can share their solutions with the entire class.

A student teacher, Scott, was surprised that a college class of twelve piano students was not very responsive to questions about the midterm performance. They played their solos for one another and Scott commented on problems and asked students how they might practice. He got very few responses to his question. Scott's next lesson was on legato pedaling and I gave him three suggestions as his supervising teacher.

- First subgroup the students into fours so they can interact more readily.
- Next tell students that they will be asked to respond to classmates' playing.
- Finally, wait longer for students to respond.

After his lecture presentation, Scott divided the class into groups of four and asked them to demonstrate and critique each other's pedaling. He roamed the room helping only when needed, and was pleased with how they worked together to understand and successfully demonstrate legato pedaling. He also had the small groups help each other with scales in flat keys through a round-robin game in which a student names a key for another student to play, then the student that played names a key for the next student to play, and so on until all have played. Scott remarked that he liked the camaraderie in the subgroups. Both students and teacher enjoyed the change of pace.

Victoria, a teacher introducing twelve-bar blues improvisation, subgrouped her piano class of music majors into groups of four. She introduced the twelve-bar blues chord progression with a right-hand improvisation of swinging eighth notes. She directed the groups to play a three-part blues arrangement, a total of four times.

- Each time, two students played a repeated rhythmic pattern using block chords, one student played a bass line using the roots of chords, and one student improvised.
- The students rotated playing a different part each time.

- The groups returned to the full class setting and performed one chorus of the blues, with each group determining who played what part.

Subgrouping effectively enabled students to learn from one another, since they heard four different approaches to playing each of the parts. By subgrouping, the frustration of not hearing themselves amongst the cacophony of twelve students improvising together was avoided. Students enjoyed learning and were successful in their performance. Victoria described her experience of the class: "Allowing the students to teach and learn from one another saves class time and the teacher's energy. At the same time, the students feel empowered in helping and critiquing others."

Students learn from one another when they listen and critique one another's playing. If the teacher makes all the corrections in a group setting, students become dependent on the teacher to do all the thinking. Teachers may assume that correcting a student's playing saves time rather than waiting for students to evaluate the playing. Yes, it does save time, but in the long run if students actively listen and evaluate playing in class, they will also do it in their practice. The group setting is an ideal one for developing habits to be used in practice.

Dividing a larger class into activity centers helps students learn, particularly if they are at different levels of advancement. In a children's class, assign each subgroup a task.

- One group plays a duet
- One group tests each other with flashcards
- One group plays a musical game.

The teacher is available to answer questions and interject comments as she travels from one group to another.

Centers also work well with college classes, particularly if they are working on different levels of the curriculum. Subgroup the students by level and assign each group a task.

- One group practices the required cadence for their level. One student plays the cadence while another names the chords being played.
- An advanced group sight reads four-part chorales in ensemble. After playing together, each plays a phrase individually without a stop between phrases.
- Another group claps and counts assigned rhythm patterns. One claps while the other evaluates.

Plan carefully so they are working together rather than individually. The creative teacher enjoys the endless possibilities for designing lessons so that peers can learn from one another.

A maxim that I always remember when a lesson lacks intensity is "When in doubt, be musical." Students are nearly always motivated when the sound is interesting. If college students are practicing scales without improving, have them play musically with a crescendo ascending and a decrescendo descending. Play together and individually and ask students to evaluate if the phrasing was heard.

A focus on expression stimulates students' imaginations so that they concentrate and play musically, yet accurately.

The teacher needs a repertoire of ways to actively engage students when a problem has been defined in a performance or a new concept has been introduced. Resources that a teacher has are the students themselves who can play, count, sing, clap, and dance to experiment with the concept being learned. Technology resources that aid the teacher are a piano laboratory with an instruction center for grouping various students together, MIDI and CD accompaniments, and computers with theory, composition, and sequencing software. Other resources are black or white boards, musical games and teaching aids including art materials, and space to move for eurhythmic activities. But the most important resources are the students.

Knowledge of the six group-dynamic principles will assist the teacher in planning group classes and allow him flexibility during the class to address issues confidently. An awareness of the principles enables the teacher to evaluate the class lesson and to take action to ensure that all students are actively participating and playing their best.

In a group lesson the teacher's role becomes one of facilitator. They listen to how the students are progressing and structure the lesson so that students listen musically and make informed decisions to improve the playing. The lesson atmosphere is fun and caring, yet productive. When students feel comfortable and confident, they recognize and appreciate their classmates playing. They become aware that learning and playing the music to the best of one's ability is the greatest reward.

Suggested Reading

Cartwright and Zander, eds., *Group Dynamics: Research and Theory.*

Further Thought

- What strategies could you use to encourage cooperation rather than competition in the group lesson?
- What advantages are there in asking students to respond to a performance rather than the teacher giving the critique?
- Think about the leader's role in both productive and non-productive groups that you have attended. What was the difference? Shared leadership? Good morale? Cooperation?

Appendix 1
Dancing the Baroque Suites

What better way to learn to play a Minuet than to dance the Minuet? We often hear piano students perfect a Minuet by increasing the tempo with each successive playing. What a revelation it would be for them to dance the stately, sophisticated steps, and with the appropriate tempo!

Imagine the clothes worn by a lady of French nobility in the early 1700s. The large powdered wig has to stay balanced while dancing, and the floor length skirt supported by a wire petticoat must stay down. A minuet tempo that is too fast may cause the dancer to lose the coiffure and to reveal one's undergarments—an embarrassing sight that most certainly would cause the court musician to look for another job!

The pianist will find, in dancing the structured steps of the Baroque suites, that the style of the dances establishes tempo, articulation, ornamentation, and phrasing. Although a piano teacher with very little dance training, I get my students off the piano bench to dance each time I assign a Baroque dance form. Without exception, they improve their performance immediately. By learning a few dance steps (walk, bend, hop, and leap), one can dance any of the suite movements of sarabande, gigue, bourée, etc. Moving to the structured steps of the sarabande, for instance, gives one a sense of pulse, meter, and phrase length that playing does not. With an awareness of the rhythmic impetus of the dance, one performs with an understanding of phrasing, articulation, and ornamentation.

You and your students may feel inhibited about dancing in a lesson. If you, as their teacher, actively participate in the movement, expect them to dance, and encourage their efforts, then students will become more relaxed. Practice combining a phrase of steps described here and repeat them throughout the suite movement. If the ballet terms are too confusing, combine steps, hops, and leaps that are characteristic of the dance.

Dancing the Baroque suite movements has consistently been one of the most enjoyable and enlightening classes for piano majors in a pedagogy course I teach on intermediate level piano literature. Teaching the steps in an individual lesson is more difficult, but possible with persistence. During a recital rehearsal on a concert hall stage, a teenage boy was having difficulty playing a gigue. I taught him the steps to the gigue, and as we hopped and leaped around the stage, he remarked, "I don't pay you to give me dance lessons!" Even though he was reluctant, after dancing the gigue, he played with much more ease and style.

Reading about the steps of the dances is not nearly as effective as learning to dance them. However, Meredith Little and Natalie Jenne give a wealth of information about Baroque music and dance steps in their book *Dance and the Music of J. S. Bach.* "The core

From Sylvia Coats, "Dancing the Baroque Suites," *Piano Life* 2, no. 1 (December 1997): 16–18. Excellence in Music, Inc. <http://www.pianovision.com> WEBZINE SHOP WPPC. Reprinted with permission.

of our approach to Baroque dance music is that rhythm and articulation form the performer's conception of phrases" (Little, 20). Most of the phrases in the dances are four to eight measures in length. The dance steps, consisting of steps and springs, give specific clues to understanding phrasing and articulation in a dance style. Turns and the position of the hands and arms add grace to the steps. A recently released video, *Baroque Dance and Baroque Keyboard Music* (Hinson), shows dancers in period dress performing all the dances. The steps are broken down so that the viewer can learn the dances.

French court dancing began in the court of Louis XIV about 1650. The graceful, elegant, and refined style was very popular in Germany. J. S. Bach composed in the style of more than twelve dance forms. Below is a synopsis of Little's description of the style of four dance forms written by Bach, the minuet, bourée, sarabande, and gigue.

The minuet is the most famous social and court dance. The character is elegant and noble, and the meter is triple. Tempo of the minuet has always been controversial and remains unsolved. Historical accounts, cited by Little, argue that in 1603 it was a gay dance and very fast, but by 1750, elegance and simplicity at a moderate tempo were noted. Probably the tempo should be no faster than ♩. = MM 42–46.

Minuet phrases are four to eight measures long in clear question-and-answer form. Slurs, attached and detached articulations can be determined by note groupings, syncopations, and harmony. Ornamentation is for expressive possibilities in the minuet. The dance steps can give clues for interpretive slurs, staccato, and ornamentation. The dance is in two-measure step units with four steps taken in six beats. Step combinations are step, bend, and rise (demi-coupés and pas marchés). Little says Minuet doubles may have been improvisations to provide more music to accompany the dance, since the original is not long enough for dancing.

The bourée has a joyful character and is played lightheartedly. Of all the dances, it is the least complex rhythmically. The meter is duple $\frac{2}{2}$, with a few in $\frac{2}{4}$, and has an upbeat. The tempo is fast compared to other French dances. The noble court bourée was slower than newer, faster bourées of the 1720s and 1730s, which were probably non-aristocratic. Metronome marking of ♩ = MM 80–88 is appropriate.

Bourée phrase lengths are four to eight measures with an upbeat. The often-seen bourée rhythm of ♩♪♪♩♩ should be articulated by phrasing the three pulses together ♩♩♪♩ ♩ or ♩♩♪♪♩♩ which gives a lilt to the music. Ornamentation is stylistically appropriate on the second beat of the third measure, just prior to the point of repose in the fourth measure. Steps are lively with combinations of springs and quick steps (pas de sissonne, jéttes chasses, and glissades).

The sarabande has a tawdry history with origins in Spain where it was accompanied by castanets and guitar. Its fiery rhythms appealed to the passionate, but by the eighteenth century it was "tamed" in the French court. The character is calm, serious, and tender with hints of passionate performance and intensity of expression. The meter is triple, either $\frac{3}{4}$ or $\frac{3}{2}$ with stress on beat two. The tempo is slow with ♩ = MM 69.

Phrases in the sarabande are balanced in four or eight measures. A typical rhythmic syncopation is ♩♩. ♪ (Little suggests the eighth be shortened to a sixteenth). In this rhythm ♩' ♩. ♪ detach beat one from a stressed beat two. Ornamentation is quite florid in the sarabande to emphasize the rhythm of the dance. Step combinations are slow and intense (temps de courante, pas coupé, pas de bourée). Little's research indicates Bach wrote more sarabandes than any other dance form and the sarabandes from the partitas are his crowning achievements in the genre.

The character of the gigue is lively and joyful. The graceful lilt is distinctive in the

French gigue, produced by the *sautillant* figure ♩. ♪ ♩ ♩. ♪ ♩ in $\frac{6}{4}$ and ♪. ♪ ♪ in $\frac{6}{8}$. Gigues have many meters—$\frac{3}{8}$, $\frac{6}{8}$, $\frac{12}{8}$, $\frac{12}{16}$, $\frac{9}{16}$, $\frac{3}{8}$. The meters share triple subdivision of the beats with duple groups. Tempo is moderate, but the gigue is the most lively of the dances. A comfortable tempo for dancing is ♩. = MM 88 in $\frac{6}{4}$ time. Phrases are balanced, imitative, and often fugal. Articulation has varied slur groupings or is in three-note groups. Very little ornamentation is used. Dance steps occur every two beats with lively hops and leaps (contretemps ballonné, pas de bourée, jettés, pas de sissonne, contretemps de gavotte).

Given the opportunity to dance the Baroque suites, students will have a physical sensation of the dance that will greatly enhance their performance.

References

Hinson, Maurice, narrator. *Baroque Dance and Baroque Keyboard Music.* Van Nuys, Calif.: Alfred Publishing Co., Inc., 1997.

Little, Meredith, and Natalie Jenne. *Dance and the Music of J. S. Bach.* Bloomington: Indiana University Press, 1991.

Here are steps used in each dance. Combine steps and repeat every four measures. The table is adapted from step descriptions by Meredith Little (Little and Jenne, pp. 22–23).

Minuet

Demi-coupés
Plié, rise onto the ball of the stepping foot.

Pas marchés
Walk on ball of foot.

Bourée

Pas de sissonne
Plié, spring from one to two feet, land plié, spring onto one foot.

Jettés chasses
Two springs from one foot to the other, with one foot chasing the other.

Glissades
Four quick steps.

Sarabande

Temps de courante
Bend on both knees, straighten and rise on the supporting foot, and slide the other foot to position slowly.

Pas coupé
Rise, walk, or glide.

Pas de bourée
Rise and two walks.

Gigue

Contretemps ballonné
Plié, hop on one foot, and leap onto the other foot.

Pas de bourée
Rise and two walks.

Jettés
Bend both knees and spring from one foot to the other.

Pas de sissonne
Plié spring from one onto two feet, land in plié, spring onto one foot, land in the following plié.

Contretemps de gavotte
Plié, hop, and two walks.

Appendix 2
Features of Court Dance of the Renaissance and Baroque Periods

Aristocrats imitated peasant dances in a more restrained and refined form. Dances were generally of two types: Basse Danse, low to the ground, and Haute Danse, high with jumping. Because of the elaborate clothing and heeled shoes worn, dancers were somewhat limited in their movements. Floor patterns were important, because the audience viewed the dance from the sides or above. The center of theatrical dance in the Baroque period was France, particularly the court of King Louis XIV at Versailles.

Court Dances

Minuet	Elegant dance performed as late as the nineteenth century. $\frac{3}{4}$ meter. Four steps in six beats.
Sarabande	Basse Danse. Spanish in origin. Religious in demeanor, grave and proud. Slow, $\frac{3}{4}$ meter. Four-measure phrases.
Bourrée	Earthy and vigorous. Has an upbeat. $\frac{2}{4}$, $\frac{2}{2}$ meters. Eight-bar phrases.
Gigue	Haute Danse. Earliest form in Italy, named after a stringed instrument, the giga. Spirited and lively, $\frac{3}{8}$, $\frac{6}{8}$, $\frac{9}{8}$, $\frac{12}{8}$ meters. Four-measure phrases.
Allemande	Basse Danse. German in origin. Slow, dignified, simple. Dancers kept hands joined throughout. $\frac{4}{4}$ meter.
Courante	Running Dance. Origins in both France and Italy. Gliding and running movements. $\frac{3}{4}$ meter.
Pavane	Basse Danse. Originated in Spain at the time of the Inquisition. Grave and religious (from the Latin meaning "peacock"). Slow tempo, walking steps. $\frac{4}{4}$ meter.
Galliard	Haute Danse. Originated in Italy (known as the Romanesa). Lively, with leaping and kicking. $\frac{3}{4}$ meter.
Gavotte	Lively and flirtatious. Has an upbeat. $\frac{2}{4}$, $\frac{2}{2}$ meters.

Suggested Sources

Hinson, *Baroque Dance and Baroque Keyboard Music.*
Krauss, Hilsendager, and Dixon, *History of the Dance in Art and Education.*
Little and Jenne, *Dance and the Music of J. S. Bach.*

Prepared by Denise A. Celestin, Associate Professor of Dance, Wichita State University

Baroque Dance Steps

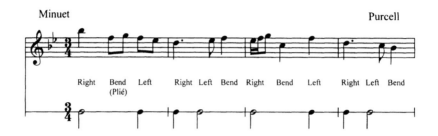

Minuet   Purcell

Right   Bend   Left   Right Left Bend Right   Bend   Left   Right Left Bend
          (Plié)

Sarabande   Handel

Sweep-Step   Rise   Sweep-Step   Rise   Step   Sweep Step   Pivot
Plié   Plié   Behind

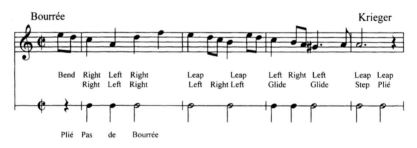

Bourrée   Krieger

Bend   Right Left Right   Leap   Leap   Left Right Left   Leap Leap
      Right Left Right   Left Right Left   Glide   Glide   Step Plié

Plié   Pas   de   Bourrée

Gigue   Telemann

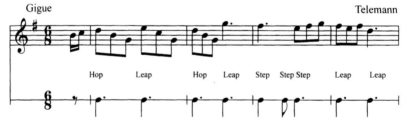

Hop   Leap   Hop   Leap   Step   Step Step   Leap   Leap

Appendix 3
Dancing and Playing
the Romantic Dances

Outline of Dance Steps

Waltz

Dance in $\frac{3}{4}$ meter, in a two-measure sequence. Elegant ballroom dance. Can be danced straight across the room, taking one half-turn per measure as shown below. On the second measure, the male does the female sequence, and vice versa, completing the second half-turn. In a simplified version of the waltz, leave out the turns.

Count		Description
Male	1	step with plié on L foot
	2	cross R foot back and pivot on ball of foot
	3	step on L foot to complete the half-turn
Female	1	step with plié on R foot
	2	step on ball of L foot
	3	step on ball of R foot to complete the half-turn

Polonaise

Polish dance in $\frac{3}{4}$ meter, in an alternating sequence. Can be done in partners, each person starting with the same leg, or with the opposite leg. Travel around the room, alternating legs.

Count	Description
1	brush R leg forward with simultaneous plié on L leg
2	step forward on ball of R foot
3	step forward on ball of L foot

Mazurka

Polish dance in $\frac{3}{4}$ meter, with stress on the second beat of the measure. In the basic mazurka step perform with weight on one leg, alternating sides. Can be choreographed adding cabrioles and turns.

Count	Description
1	step forward on R foot with plié (L foot ready to brush)
2	hop on R while brushing L foot, extending leg forward
3	hop (chug) forward on R foot in plié

Czardas

Hungarian dance in duple meter. Starts with a slow section (shown below). May be performed straight forward, or side to side. Then it changes to a brisk tempo, including backward skips, stamping/clapping, pas de bourrées, and cabrioles.

Count	Description	Arm
1	step in deep plié on R, dragging L foot slightly	R hand behind head
2	kick L leg forward with small hop on R foot	R arm extends
3	step forward on L foot	
4	step forward on R foot	

Suggested Reading

Aldrich, *From the Ballroom to Hell: Grace and Folly in Nineteenth-Century Dance.*
Teten, *Dancetime! 500 Years of Social Dance.*

Prepared by Denise A. Celestin, Associate Professor of Dance, Wichita State University

Bibliography

Albergo, Cathy, and Reid Alexander. *Intermediate Piano Repertoire*. 4th ed. Mississauga, Ontario, Canada: The Frederick Harris Music Co., 2000.

Aldrich, Elizabeth. *From the Ballroom to Hell: Grace and Folly in Nineteenth-Century Dance*. Evanston, Ill.: Northwestern University Press, 1991.

American College of Musicians. 2004. American College of Musicians. 6 August 2004 <http://www.pianoguild.com/>.

Anderson, Richard Paul. "Skip the Opening Lecture and Play." *Clavier* 39, no. 4 (April 2000): 6–8.

Andre, Thomas, and Gary D. Phye, eds. *Cognitive Classroom Learning*. New York: Academic Press, 1986.

Associated Board of the Royal Schools of Music. 2004. The Associated Board of the Royal Schools of Music. 10 August 2004 <http://www.abrsm.ac.uk/>.

Baker-Jordan, Martha. *Practical Piano Pedagogy, the Definitive Text for Piano Teachers and Pedagogy Students*. Miami, Fla.: Warner Brothers Publications, 2003.

Barbe, Walter, and Raymond Swassing. *The Swassing-Barbe Modality Index*. Columbus, Ohio: Zaner-Bloser, 1979.

———. *Teaching through Modality Strengths: Concepts and Practices*. Columbus, Ohio: Zaner-Bloser, 1979.

Barnes, Douglas, and Frankie Todd. *Communication and Learning Revisited: Making Meaning through Talk*. Portsmouth: Boyton/Cook Publishers, 1995.

Bastien, James W., and E. Gregory Nagode. *How to Teach Piano Successfully*. 3rd ed. San Diego, Calif.: Neil A. Kjos Music Co., 1988.

Bernstein, Seymour. *With Your Own Two Hands*. New York: G. Schirmer, 1981.

Booth, David, and Carol Thornley-Hall, eds. *Classroom Talk*. Portsmouth, N.H.: Heinemann Educational Books, 1991.

Bruner, Jerome. *The Process of Education*. Cambridge, Mass.: Harvard University Press, 1960.

Caldwell, J. Timothy. *Expressive Singing: Dalcroze Eurhythmics for Voice*. Englewood Cliffs, N.J.: Prentice Hall, 1995.

Camp, Max W. *Developing Piano Performance*. Chapel Hill, N.C.: Hinshaw Music, 1981.

Cartwright, Dorwin, and Alvin Zander, eds. *Group Dynamics: Research and Theory*. 3rd ed. New York: Harper & Row, 1968.

Coats, Sylvia. *A Correlational Study of Aesthetic Piano Performance and a Learning Approach Based on a Gestalt Theory of Problem Solving*. D.M.A. dissertation. Ann Arbor, Mich.: University Microfilms, 1978.

———. "Count and Move Out Loud." *Piano Guild Notes* 41, no. 3 (November/December 1991): 4–5.

———. "Dancing the Baroque Suites." *Piano Life* 2, no. 1 (December 1997): 16–18.

———, Rebecca Shockley, Sandra L. Camp, and Marvin Blickenstaff, eds. "The Heart of the Matter: Rhythm." *Keyboard Companion* 2, no. 1 (Spring 1991): 30–32.

Covey, Stephen R. *The Seven Habits of Highly Effective People: Restoring the Character Ethic*. New York: Simon and Schuster, 1989.

Csikszentmihalyi, Mihaly, Kevin Rathunde, and Samuel Whalen. *Talented Teenagers: The Roots of Success and Failure.* New York: Cambridge University Press, 1993.

Deutsch, Morton. "The Effects of Cooperation and Competition upon Group Process." In *Group Dynamics: Research and Theory,* ed. Dorwin Cartwright and Alvin Zander. 3rd ed. New York: Harper & Row, 1968. 461–482.

Dewey, John. *The School and Society* (1900) and *The Child and the Curriculum* (1902). Chicago: University of Chicago Press, 1990.

Duckworth, Guy. "Group Lessons for Advanced Students with No Private Lessons," and "Group Dynamics." In *Proceedings from Pedagogy Saturday III.* Cincinnati, Ohio: Music Teachers National Association, 1999. 16–18, 57–59, 78–79.

——. "Fingering Logic." *Clavier* 1, no. 2 (1962): 16–19.

——. *Keyboard Explorer.* Evanston, Ill.: M-F Music, div. of Opus Music Publishers, 1980.

——. "Keyboard Literacy." *Clavier* 1, no. 1 (1962): 24, 26, 28.

——. *Keyboard Musician,* Book VI: *The Symmetrical Keyboard, Pedagogical Perspectives for the Twenty-First Century.* Rev. ed. Denver, Colo.: Group Environments Press, 1990.

——. "Notes on Group Performance Instruction in the Studio." In *Proceedings of the Forty-Ninth Annual Meeting of the National Association of the Schools of Music,* 1974. 97–106.

——, with Sylvia Coats. ". . . Reflections." *American Music Teacher* 54, no. 1 (August/ September 2004): 41–42.

——. "What Are We Teaching—Concepts or Details?" *Clavier* 3, no. 3 (1964): 45, 46, 50.

Duke, Robert A. *Intelligent Music Teaching: Essays on the Core Principles of Effective Instruction.* Austin, Tex.: Learning and Behavior Resources, 2005.

——. "Teachers' Verbal Corrections and Observers' Perceptions of Teaching and Learning." *Journal of Research in Music Education* 50, no. 1 (2002): 75–87.

Fink, Seymour. *Mastering Piano Technique: A Guide for Students, Teachers and Performers.* Portland, Ore.: Amadeus Press, 1992.

Flanders, Ned A. *Analyzing Teaching Behavior.* Reading, Mass.: Addison-Wesley Publishing Co., 1970.

Ganz, Rudolph. *Exercises for Piano, Contemporary and Special.* Evanston, Ill.: Summy-Birchard Co., 1967.

Gardner, Howard. *Frames of Mind: The Theory of Multiple Intelligences.* New York: Basic Books, 1983.

"Getting Started in Group Teaching." Video. Dallas: National Piano Foundation, 2001.

Gigante, Beth. *A Business Guide for the Music Teacher.* San Diego, Calif.: Neil A. Kjos Music Co., 1987.

Golay, Keith. *Learning Patterns and Temperament Styles.* Fullerton, Calif.: Manas-Systems, 1982.

Green, Barry, and Phyllis Lehrer. *The Inner Game of Music Solo Workbook for Piano.* Chicago, Ill.: GIA Publications, 1995.

Hinson, Maurice, narrator. Dir. Christopher Hepp. *Baroque Dance and Baroque Keyboard Music.* Van Nuys, Calif.: Alfred Publishing Co., 1997.

Hinson, Maurice. *Guide to the Pianist's Repertoire.* 3rd ed. Bloomington: Indiana University Press, 2000.

Jaques-Dalcroze, Émile. *Rhythm, Music, and Education.* Trans. Harold F. Rubenstein. London: The Dalcroze Society, 1972.

Keirsey, David, and Marilyn Bates. *Please Understand Me: Character and Temperament Types.* 4th ed. Del Mar, Calif.: Prometheus Nemesis Book Company, 1984.

Krauss, Richard, Sarah Chapman Hilsendager, and Brenda Dixon. *History of the Dance in Art and Education.* 3rd ed. Englewood Cliffs, N.J.: Prentice Hall, 1991.

Kropff, Kris, ed. *A Symposium for Pianists and Teachers: Strategies to Develop the Mind and Body for Optimal Performance.* Dayton, Ohio: Heritage Music Press, 2002.

Lawrence, Gordon. *People Types and Tiger Stripes: A Practical Guide to Learning Styles.* 2nd ed. Gainesville, Fla.: Center for Applications of Psychological Type, 1982.

Little, Meredith, and Natalie Jenne. *Dance and the Music of J. S. Bach.* Bloomington: Indiana University Press, 1991.

Magrath, Jane. *The Pianist's Guide to Standard Teaching and Performance Literature.* Van Nuys, Calif.: Alfred Publishing Co., 1995.

Mursell, James L. *Education for Musical Growth.* New York: Ginn and Company, 1948.

Music Teachers National Association. 2004. Music Teachers National Association. 5 August 2004 <http://www.mtna.org/>.

Myers, Isabel Briggs, with Peter B. Myers. *Gifts Differing.* Palo Alto, Calif.: Consulting Psychologists Press, 1980.

Nystrand, Martin. *Opening Dialogue: Understanding the Dynamics of Language and Learning in the English Classroom.* New York: Teachers College Press, 1997.

"Pedagogy Saturday VI, Exploring Learning Styles: Developing a Flexible Teaching Approach," *American Music Teacher* 52, no. 2 (October/November, 2002): 23–55.

Piaget, Jean, and Barbel Inhelder. *The Psychology of the Child.* Trans. Helen Weaver. New York: Basic Books, 1969.

Piano Pedagogy Forum. 1 July 2004. Piano Pedagogy Forum. 9 August 2004 <http://music.sc.edu/ea/keyboard/ppf/>.

"Piano Syllabus 2003–2005." *Trinity the International Examination Board.* 2004. Trinity College London. 4 June 2004 <http://www.trinitycollege.co.uk/>.

Pianonet. 2004. National Piano Foundation. 9 August 2004 <http://pianonet.com/>.

Proceedings from Pedagogy Saturday III. Seminar theme: "Three or More: Beyond the Traditional Private Lesson." Cincinnati, Ohio: Music Teachers National Association, 1999.

Proceedings from Pedagogy Saturday IV. Seminar theme: "One-on-One and Three-or-More Teaching." Cincinnati, Ohio: Music Teachers National Association, 2000.

RCM Examinations. 2004. RCM Examinations. 4 August 2004 <http://www.rcmexaminations.org/>.

Royal American Conservatory Examinations. 2004. Royal American Conservatory Examinations. 25 June 2004 <http://www.royalamericanconservatory.org/>.

Schnebly-Black, Julia, and Stephen F. Moore. *Rhythm: One on One—Dalcroze Activities in the Private Music Lesson.* Van Nuys, Calif.: Alfred Publishing Co., 2004.

Serafine, Mary Louise. *Music as Cognition: The Development of Thought in Sound.* New York: Columbia University Press, 1988.

Shockley, Rebecca Payne. *Mapping Music: For Faster Learning and Secure Memory.* Madison, Wis.: A-R Editions, 1997.

Teten, Carol, artistic director. *Dancetime! 500 Years of Social Dance.* Kentfield, Calif.: Dancetime Publications, 1998.

Trinity the International Examination Board. 2004. Trinity College London. 4 June 2004 <http://www.trinitycollege.co.uk/>.

Uszler, Marienne, Stewart Gordon, and Scott McBride Smith. *The Well-Tempered Keyboard Teacher.* 2nd ed. New York: Schirmer Books, 2000.

Westney, William. *The Perfect Wrong Note: Learning to Trust Your Musical Self.* Pompton Plains, N.J.: Amadeus Press, 2003.

Index

accepting feelings, 74, 75, 78–79
accidentals, 37, 50
accompanying, 129
activity centers, 144
aesthetic concepts, 29–30, 32, 40–44
Albergo, Cathy, 57
aleatoric music, 39
Alexander, Reid, 57
allemande, 151
Allison, Irl, 66
American College of Musicians, 66
analogous activities, 6, 7, 11–13, 17, 125, 131;
     eurhythmic activities, 23–24
analysis, interaction, 71, 74–77, 90
analysis of music, 20, 23
approach: in group lessons, 117–118, 121–122;
     lesson planning and, 5, 6, 13–14, 17; read-
     ing, 59–60; technique, 60; top-down, 19–
     20, 54
arsis, 51
articulation, 29, 30, 32, 41–43, 148
articulation principle, 49–50
assessment, 61–69; MTNA Assessment Tools
     for the Independent Music Teacher, 67–68
Associated Board of the Royal Schools of
     Music, 67
attendance policy, 139
auditions, 108–110
auditory learning, 94–96
aural reading, 33
aural testing, 108
awareness, structural, 29

Bach, Johann Sebastian, 42, 49–50, 148
Baker-Jordan, Martha, 57
Barbe, Walter, 94–95, 96
Baroque Dance and Baroque Keyboard Music
     (Hinson), 148
Baroque dance forms, 24, 50, 151–152
Baroque suites, 147–150
basic concepts, 29–30, 31, 33–40
Basse Danse, 151
behavior, 123, 140–142
bench height, 45, 60
blame, 108

bourée, 50, 148–149, 151, 152
Brahms, Johannes, 42, 43
Briggs, Katherine, 96
Bruner, Jerome, 19, 20, 29, 54
building on student's ideas, 74, 75, 81–83

care and nurture of the piano student, 16–18
Cartwright, Dorwin, 134
categories of interaction, 74–77, 89
challenge, 117, 118–119
Champagne, David, 100
checklist for teaching, 16–18
children, 123, 125; group lessons, 108, 109,
     116; as naturally intuitive, 19–20
clapping exercises, 23–24, 35, 130
clef signs, 33
cognitive growth, stages of, 20
college class piano curriculum, 61–65
communication, 2, 5; accepting feelings, 74,
     75, 78–79; balanced pattern, 71–72, 74, 77,
     91–92; building on student's ideas, 74, 75,
     81–83; criticizing and justifying authority,
     74, 76, 88–89; direct and indirect influences,
     74–77; doing *vs.* telling, 13, 14; dominative
     vs. integrative approach, 71–72; giving direc-
     tions, 74, 76, 87–88; group dynamics and,
     135; lecturing, 74, 76, 86–87; lesson plan-
     ning and, 5, 14; patterns of influence, 90–
     92; praising and encouraging, 74, 75, 80–81,
     88; questions and, 14, 74, 75–76, 83–86; si-
     lence, 77, 90; student responses, 89–90
competence, musical, 20
competition, group dynamics and, 139,
     140–142
complexity of knowledge, 55–56
composition, 117
comprehension, 54, 55
concepts, 28, 58; aesthetic, 29–30, 32, 40–44;
     articulation, 29, 30, 32, 41–43, 148; basic,
     29–30, 31, 33–40; as basis for curriculum,
     58; contrasting, 120; dynamics, 40–41;
     form, 38–39; group activities for learning,
     130–131; group lessons and, 9–10, 117–118,
     120–122; guidebook for teaching, 30–33; les-
     son planning and, 4–6, 8–11, 16, 120–122;

limiting, 120–121; pitch, 33–34; rhythm, 34–36; scale, 30, 31, 37–38; technique, 29–30, 32, 44–47; tempo, 44; tension and release, 39–40; texture, 36–37; topography, 30, 32, 46–47

conceptual memory, 54–55

conducting, 130

contextual learning, 54

continuity transfer, 53

cooperative learning, 4, 5; group dynamics and, 135, 139–142

corrections, 4–5, 21–22, 86, 88–89; critical thinking skills and, 25–26; criticizing and justifying authority, 74, 76; questions and, 83–84

courante, 151

Covey, Stephen, 71

crescendo and decrescendo, 40–41, 51, 58

critical pattern of influence, 90–91

critical thinking, 4, 24–27

criticizing, justifying authority, 74, 76, 88–89

Csikszentmihalyi, Mihaly, 3

curriculum, 2, 5, 8, 57; building, 61–63; comprehensive, 57–58; content, 60–61; improvisation and, 55, 61–65; levels of development, 62–63; methods and, 58–59, 60; reading approach, 59–60; spiral, 57; technique approach, 60

Dalcroze Method, 35

Dance and the Music of J. S. Bach (Little and Jenne), 147–148

dance forms, 2, 35; Baroque, 24, 50, 151–152; Renaissance, 151–152; Romantic, 153–154

dependency on teacher, 4–5, 21, 73, 91, 135

digital piano laboratory, 143

direct influences, 74–76

directions, giving, 74, 76, 87–88

discussion approach, 5, 72

dominative influence, 71–72

Duckworth, Guy, 21, 33, 58, 71, 112

duets, 137

dynamics, 29, 32, 39–41, 45, 52–53

ear training, 33, 59

educated guesses, 2, 19–21

elementary level students, objectives for, 6–7

emotions, 19, 73; accepting feelings, 74, 75, 78–79; effect of music on, 19, 29, 41; group growth and, 113, 114, 115; rhythm and, 34–35

empathy, 73, 79

encouragement, 74, 75, 80–81, 88

etudes, 45

eurhythmics, 23–24, 35–36, 130–131, 140; reading approach and, 59–60

evaluation, 5, 6, 15, 135

exams, 63–69, 138, 139

exercises, technical, 45–47, 53

experience, concrete/direct, 6, 20; group lessons and, 117, 118, 120; lesson planning for, 11–13, 17

extraversion-introversion preference, 96–97

facilitators, teachers as, 106–107, 133–134, 137, 145

feedback, 3, 73, 136

fingering, 32, 46–47

Flanders, Ned, 71–72, 74

flow model, 3

form, 30, 31, 38–39

functional skills, 6, 24, 58, 117, 118, 125–128, 137

galliard, 151

Gardner, Howard, 20

gavotte, 151

generalizations, 49, 123. *See also* musical principles

get-acquainted meetings, 94

gigue, 148–149, 151, 152

goals, 3

grand staff, 34, 59, 121

group dynamics, 133–134; competition and, 139, 140–142; group as medium of change, 135, 142–145; individual responsibility, 133, 135, 138–139; inhibitions and self-esteem, 135, 136–138; misbehavior and, 140–142; mistakes and, 136, 137, 139–140; participatory leadership, 134–135; principles of, 135; spirit of cooperation, 135, 139–142. *See also* group lessons

group growth: emotions and, 113, 114, 115; individual differences, 113, 114–115; influence, 112–113, 114, 115; membership, 112, 114; motivation, 115–116; productivity, 113–114, 115; stages of, 112, 113–114. *See also* group lessons

group lessons, 2, 18; accepting feelings, 79; asking questions, 85, 117, 119; auditions, 108–110; children, 108, 109, 116; classroom management, 123; college students, 108, 110; concepts and, 9–10, 117–118, 120–122; cooperative learning, 13, 135, 139–142; experience and, 117, 118, 120; homogeneous placement of students, 106, 107–111, 141; improvisation and, 124, 125, 126–127, 136; known to unknown progression, 118–119;

lecturing, 86; morale and, 138–139; motivation and, 115–116, 117, 118, 128–129; subgrouping classes, 143–145; teach to prepared student, 119; tests, 138, 139; transfer of concepts, 117, 118, 123–125. *See also* group growth; group problem solving
group problem solving: challenge, level of, 117, 118–119; functional skills, 125–128; group activities for learning concepts, 130–131; limiting conditions, 117, 118, 120–123; motivation, 128–129; musical principles and, 123–125
guessing and exploration, 19–20

hand position, 45, 46, 124
harmonic rhythm, 35–36
harmonization, 11, 125–126, 137
harmony, tonic and dominant, 39, 124–125
Haute Danse, 151
headphones, 136–137, 142, 143
Hinson, Maurice, 57
history, 28–29
Hogan, R. Craig, 100

imaginative associations, 41, 44
improvisation, 11–12, 33, 124, 125, 126–127, 129, 136; conceptual memory and, 54–55; curriculum and, 55, 61–65; modes and, 123–124
indirect influences, 74–77
individual responsibility, group dynamics and, 133, 135, 138–139
influence, 17; direct *vs.* indirect, 74–77; group growth and, 112–113, 114, 115; integrative, 71–72; patterns of, 90–92
inhibitions, 135, 137–138
integrative influence, 71–72
intelligence, types of, 20
intensity of purpose, 15
interaction, categories of, 74, 75–77, 89
interaction analysis, 71, 74–77, 89; intermediate level students, 8–9, 26
Intermediate Piano Repertoire (Albergo and Alexander), 57
interpretation, 2, 27, 29, 51–52
intervallic reading, 33, 58, 59
intuitive thinking, 11–13, 17, 19–20, 26, 97; student discovery and, 22–24

Jaques-Dalcroze, Émile, 35
Jenne, Natalie, 147–148, 149
judging-perceiving preference, 98
Jung, Carl, 96

Kansas Music Teachers Association, 65–66, 68–69
key signature, 37
Keyboard Explorer (Duckworth), 125
kinesthetic learning, 35, 95–96
known to unknown progression, 118–119

leadership, participatory, 134–135
learning, rhythm of, 20–22
learning modalities, 2, 94–96
learning styles, 2, 5, 14–15, 94, 107
lecturing, 74, 76, 86–87
lesson planning, 2, 3; analogies, 7, 12–13; approach, 5, 6, 13–14, 17; communication and, 5, 14; concepts and, 4–6, 8–11, 16, 120–122; concrete experience and, 11–13, 17; evaluation, 5, 6, 15; group lessons, 18; learning styles and, 5, 14–15; materials, 5, 6, 7–8, 16; objectives of lesson, 5–7; pacing, 5, 15; theory and history in lesson, 28–29
limiting conditions, 11, 13, 17, 22–23, 53; group lessons and, 117, 118, 120–123
listening skills, 23–24, 33, 59, 130
Little, Meredith, 147–148, 149
Louis XIV, 148, 151

Magrath, Jane, 57
marking, 123
materials, 5, 6, 7–8, 16
mazurka, 153
melody, 20
memory, conceptual, 54–55
meter, 29, 38, 40, 130–131
methods, 6–7, 16, 53; concepts and, 8–9; curriculum and, 58–59, 60
metrical organization, 39–40
minuet, 147, 148, 151, 152
mirroring, 127–128
misbehavior, in group lessons, 140–142
mistakes, 21–22, 136, 137, 139–140
modes, 37–38, 46–47, 122–124
modulation, 50–51
morale of group, 138–139
motivation, 139; group lessons and, 115–116, 117, 118, 128–129
movement, 20, 23–24. *See also* eurhythmics
Mursell, James, 3, 20–21
Music Achievement Award Program, MTNA, 68
music majors, 108, 110, 114–116, 128–129, 137
Music Progressions (Kansas Music Teachers Association), 65–66, 68–69
Music Teachers National Association (MTNA), 65, 67–68
musical intelligence, 20

musical principles, 2, 29, 47, 49; advantages of teaching, 53–56; articulation, 49–50; group lessons and, 117, 118; group problem solving and, 123–125; phrasing, 51; tonality, 50–51

Myers, Isabel, 96

Myers-Briggs Type Indicator, 96–104; common types, 98; matching types, 98; piano pedagogy student types, 100–101; student-teacher comments, 101–104; type teaching examples, 98–100

Myers-Briggs type theory, 2

notation, 121

objectives, 5, 6–7

open-ended questions, 83, 89

ornamentation, 148

pacing, 5, 15

pavane, 151

pedagogy students, 68–69, 100–104

pedaling, 42–43

performance, 1, 130

performance classes, 138

Personal Style Inventory, 100

personality type, 96–100

phrasing, 29, 37, 38, 39–40

phrasing principles, 51–52

physical tension, 45–46, 53, 124

Piaget, Jean, 20

The Pianist's Guide to Standard Teaching and Performance Literature (Magrath), 57

Piano Guild, 66–67

Pieczonka, Albert, 53

pitch, 29–30, 31, 33–34

playing by ear, 33, 59, 127

polonaise, 153

positive comments, 140

posture, 44–45

Practical Piano Pedagogy (Baker-Jordan), 57

praising, encouraging, 74, 75, 80–81, 88

principle formation, 49. See also musical principles

probing questions, 83

problem solving, 4–5, 16, 24–27, 117. See also group problem solving

process, 1–2

productivity, 113–114, 115, 139

professional development, 1–2

pulse, 35, 44, 53, 59, 130

question-answer pattern of influence, 91

questions, 5, 14, 23, 73–76, 82–86; asked by

student, 77, 84, 89; for functional skills, 125–126; group lessons and, 85, 117, 119

reading approach, 59–60

reading music, 33–34, 59–60, 131; intervallic approach, 33, 58

recording of lessons, 73, 74

Renaissance court dance, 151

repertoire, 57

repetitive motion syndrome, 45

rhythm, 29–30, 31, 34–36, 130

rhythm of learning, 20–22

rhythmic approach to reading, 59

risk taking, 2

Romantic dances, 153–154

Royal American Conservatory Examinations (RACE), 67

Royal Conservatory of Music (RCM), 67

rubato, 44

sarabande, 148, 149, 151, 152

sautillant figure, 149

scale, 30, 31, 37–38, 46, 50

self-esteem, 135, 136–138

sensing-intuition preference, 97

sensory perception, modes of, 94–96

Seven Habits of Highly Effective People (Covey), 71

silence, 77, 90

similarities between compositions, 28, 50, 118

simplification, 121

singing, 23, 33, 59, 108

skills: concepts and, 11, 17; functional, 24, 58, 117, 118, 125–128, 137; symmetry of, 6, 13, 23–24

Smith, Scott McBride, 67

social psychology, 1, 134

sonata form, 39, 50–51

sound, features of, 20

spiral curriculum, 57

structure, 2, 54–56

structure of subject matter, 29, 57

student discovery: analysis of music, 20, 23; guessing and exploration, 19–21; intuitive thinking, 22–24; problem solving/critical thinking, 24–27; rhythm of learning, 20–22

students: aspirations, 3; building on ideas of, 74, 75, 81–83; care and nurture of, 16–18; dependency on teacher, 4–5, 21, 73, 91, 135; lack of progress, 73, 79, 81; level of understanding, 57; music majors, 108, 110, 114–116, 128–129, 137; participation, 74, 77; process of, 2; as resources, 1, 145; responses, 89–90; responsibility of, 133, 135, 138–139;

transfer, 106, 107–108; as unique individuals, 1, 3, 26–27; verbalization of ideas, 22, 81. *See also* group lessons

style, 131

style periods, 13

Swassing, Raymond, 94–95, 96

Swassing-Barbe Modality Index, 96

symmetry of skills, 6, 13, 23–24

A Symposium for Pianists and Teachers: Strategies to Develop the Mind and Body for Optimal Performance (Kropff, ed.), 44

"Tarantella" (Pieczonka), 53

teachers: comments made by, in group, 139–140; experience level, 1–2; as facilitators, 106–107, 133–134, 137, 145; influence of, 17, 71–72, 74–77, 90–92, 112–114

technique, 30, 32, 44–46, 131

technique approach, 60

technique concepts, 29–30, 32, 44–47

technique transfer, 53

technology, use of, 14, 17, 63–65, 145

tempo, 30, 32, 44

tension and release, 30, 31, 39–40, 51

texture, 30, 31, 36–37

theory, 28–29

thesis, 51

thinking-feeling preference, 97–98

time signatures, 35

tonal center, 37

tonality principle, 50–51

tonic and dominant harmony, 39, 124–125

top-down approach, 19–20, 54

topography, 30, 32, 46–47

transfer of concepts, 17, 49, 52–53, 55, 58; group lessons and, 117, 118, 123–125

transfer students, 106, 107–108

transposition, 11, 30, 58, 59, 87–88, 126

triad inversions, 125–126

Trinity College London, 68

trust, 88–89

tuition, 138

understanding, 123–124

Uszler, Marienne, 25, 57

verbalization of concepts, 22, 81

verification of problem, 25–26, 117, 123

visual imagery, dynamics and, 41

visual learning, 94–96

waltz, 153

The Well-Tempered Keyboard Teacher (Uszler), 25, 57

wrist movement, 45, 124

SYLVIA COATS is Professor of Piano Pedagogy and Class Piano at Wichita State University. She is an active member of Music Teachers National Association and has served on the board of directors. She has presented lectures throughout the United States and China, and performs with the Wichita Symphony Orchestra and the Sotto Voce Trio. She holds bachelor's and master's degrees in piano performance from Texas Tech University and a D.M.A. degree in performance and pedagogy from the University of Colorado.

CPSIA information can be obtained at www.ICGtesting.com
Printed in the USA
LVOW090346130112

263699LV00002B/10/P